中国成语故事 *Chinese Idiom Stories*

王双双　编著

图书在版编目（CIP）数据

中国成语故事 / 王双双编著. —2版.—北京：北京大学出版社，2016.10（2022.1重印）
（新双双中文教材）
ISBN 978-7-301-27563-4

Ⅰ.①中… Ⅱ.①王… Ⅲ.①汉语—成语—对外汉语教学—教材 Ⅳ.①H195.4

中国版本图书馆CIP数据核字（2016）第224791号

书　　　名	中国成语故事（第二版）
	ZHONGGUO CHENGYU GUSHI
著作责任者	王双双　编著
英文翻译	［德］Nanny Kim（金兰中）
责任编辑	邓晓霞
标准书号	ISBN 978-7-301-27563-4
出版发行	北京大学出版社
地　　　址	北京市海淀区成府路205号　100871
网　　　址	http://www.pup.cn　　新浪微博：@北京大学出版社
电子信箱	zpup@pup.cn
电　　　话	邮购部 62752015　发行部 62750672　编辑部 62767349
印刷者	三河市博文印刷有限公司
经销者	新华书店
	889毫米×1194毫米　16开本　9.25印张　83千字
	2006年7月第1版
	2016年10月第2版　2022年3月第4次印刷
定　　　价	76.00元（含课本、练习本、手工作业）

未经许可，不得以任何方式复制或抄袭本书之部分或全部内容。
版权所有，侵权必究
举报电话：010-62752024　电子信箱：fd@pup.pku.edu.cn
图书如有印装质量问题，请与出版部联系，电话：010-62756370

第二版序

能够与北京大学出版社合作出版"双双中文教材"的第二版，让这套优秀的对外汉语教材泽被更多的学生，加州中文教学研究中心备感荣幸。

这是一套洋溢着浓浓爱意的教材。作者的女儿在美国出生，到了识字年龄，作者教她学习过市面上流行的多套中文教材，但都强烈地感觉到这些教材"水土不服"。一解女儿学习中文的燃眉之急，是作者编写这套教材的初衷和原动力。为了让没有中文环境的孩子能够喜欢学习中文，作者字斟句酌地编写课文；为了赋予孩子审美享受、引起他们的共鸣，作者特邀善画儿童创作了一幅幅稚气可爱的插图；为了加深孩子们对内容的理解，激发孩子们的学习热情，作者精心设计了充满创造性的互动活动。

这是一套承载着文化传承使命感的教材。语言不仅仅是文化的载体，更是文化重要的有机组成部分。学习一门外语的深层障碍往往根植于目标语言与母语间的文化差异。这种差异对于学习中文的西方学生尤为突出。这套教材的使用对象正处在好奇心和好胜心最强的年龄阶段，作者抓住了这一特点，变阻力为动力，一改过去削学生认知能力和智力水平之"足"以适词汇和语言知识之"履"的通病。教材在高年级部分，一个学期一个文化主题，以对博大精深的中国文化的探索激发学生的学习兴趣，使学生在学习语言的同时了解璀璨的中国文化。

"双双中文教材"自2005年面世以来，受到了老师、学生和家长的广泛欢迎。很多觉得中文学习枯燥无味而放弃的学生，因这套教材发现了学习中文的乐趣，又重新回到了中文课堂。本次修订，作者不仅吸纳了老师们对于初版的反馈意见和自己实际使用过程中的心得，还参考了近年对外汉语教学理论及实践方面的成果。语言学习部分由原来的九册改为五册，一学年学习一册，文化学习部分保持一个专题一册。相信修订后的"新双双中文教材"会更方便、实用，让更多学生受益。

张晓江
美国加州中文教学研究中心秘书长

第一版前言

"双双中文教材"是一套专门为海外青少年编写的中文课本，是我在美国八年的中文教学实践基础上编写成的。在介绍这套教材之前，请读一首小诗：

> 一双神奇的手，
> 推开一扇窗。
> 一条神奇的路，
> 通向灿烂的中华文化。

鲍凯文　鲍维江

鲍维江和鲍凯文姐弟俩是美国生美国长的孩子，也是我的学生。1998年冬，他们送给我的新年贺卡上的小诗，深深地打动了我的心。我把这首诗看成我文化教学的"回声"。我要传达给海外每位中文老师：我教给他们（学生）中国文化，他们思考了、接受了、回应了。这条路走通了！

语言是一种交流的工具，更是一种文化和一种生活方式，所以学习中文也就离不开中华文化的学习。汉字是一种古老的象形文字，她从远古走来，带有大量的文化信息，但学起来并不容易。使学生增强兴趣、减小难度，走出苦学汉字的怪圈，走进领悟中华文化的花园，是我编写这套教材的初衷。

学生不论大小，天生都有求知的欲望，都有欣赏文化美的追求。中华文化本身是魅力十足的。把这宏大而玄妙的文化，深入浅出地，有声有色地介绍出来，让这迷人的文化如涓涓细流，一点一滴地渗入学生们的心田，使学生们逐步体味中国文化，是我编写这套教材的目的。

为此我将汉字的学习放入文化介绍的流程之中同步进行，让同学们在学中国地理的同时，学习汉字；在学中国历史的同时，学习汉字；在学中国哲学的同时，学习汉字；在学中国科普文选的同时，学习汉字……

这样的一种中文学习，知识性强，趣味性强；老师易教，学生易学。当学生们合上书本时，他们的眼前是中国的大好河山，是中国五千年的历史和妙不可言的哲学思维，是奔腾的现代中国……

总之，他们了解了中华文化，就会探索这片土地，热爱这片土地，就会与中国结下情缘。

最后我要衷心地感谢所有热情支持和帮助我编写教材的老师、家长、学生、朋友和家人。特别是老同学唐玲教授、何茜老师和我女儿Uta Guo年复一年的鼎力相助。可以说这套教材是大家努力的结果。

王双双

课程设置（建议）

序号	书名	适用年级
1	中文课本　第一册	幼儿园/一年级
2	中文课本　第二册	二年级
3	中文课本　第三册	三年级
4	中文课本　第四册	四年级
5	中文课本　第五册	五年级
6	中国成语故事	六年级
7	中国地理常识	六年级
8	中国古代故事	七年级
9	中国神话传说	七年级
10	中国古代科学技术	八年级
11	中国民俗与民间艺术	八年级
12	中国文学欣赏	九年级
13	中国诗歌欣赏	九年级
14	中国古代哲学	十年级
15	中国历史	十年级

目 录

第一课	守株待兔	1
第二课	拔苗助长	2
第二课	画蛇添足	8
第三课	狐假虎威	13
	自相矛盾	14
第四课	滥竽充数	19
第五课	鹬蚌相争	25
第六课	胸有成竹	31
	竹文化	32
第七课	望梅止渴	38
第八课	塞翁失马	44
第九课	伯乐相马	51
第十课	愚公移山	57
生字表（简）		64
生字表（繁）		65
生词表（简）		66
生词表（繁）		68
附录 "新双双中文教材"写作练习（1—6册）		70

第一课

守株待兔

春秋时期①，宋国②有个农夫。一天，他正在地里劳动，忽然看见一只兔子飞跑过来。兔子跑得太快，不小心撞到地里的一棵大树上，撞死了。农夫非常高兴，跑过去捡起这只死兔子，拿回家美美地吃了一顿。他一边吃一边想：这样就有兔子吃，多省力啊。我不用天天在地里劳动了！于是他不再干活，拿了一个大

---

① 春秋时期——中国历史上的一个时期（前770年—前476年）。
② 宋国——中国春秋时期的一个诸侯(zhū hóu)国。

^{kuāng}
筐，守在树下，等着兔子来。但是他等了一天又一天，什么也没有等到，他的田地却因为没有人种，长满了草。大家看他不种地，天天等兔子，都笑话他。

后来，人们就用成语"守株待兔"比喻不努力还想成功。

拔苗助长

春秋时期，有一个农夫，种了一片禾苗。第二天他见禾苗没有长高，心里有点儿着急。第三天他见禾苗还没有长高，心里更着急了，于是就把禾苗一棵一棵地都拔高了一点儿。到了第四天，他到田里一看，所有的禾苗都死了。

后来，人们就用"拔苗助长"比喻只按自己的想法做事，急
^{ér}
于求成，反而坏事。

生词

守株待兔	shǒu zhū dài tù	guarding the tree trunk to wait for rabbits
时期	shí qī	period
宋	sòng	Song (*name of a state; surname*)
农夫	nóng fū	farmer, peasant
劳动	láo dòng	work; labor
忽然	hū rán	suddenly
撞	zhuàng	crash
省力	shěng lì	spare the effort
笑话	xiào hua	joke
成语	chéng yǔ	chengyu, four-character idiom
比喻	bǐ yù	metaphor
成功	chéng gōng	success; succeed
拔苗助长	bá miáo zhù zhǎng	pulling at the seedlings to help them grow
更	gèng	more

听写

守株待兔　拔苗助长　时期　宋　农夫　劳动　忽然　笑话　成语　更　*撞到　省力

比一比

夫 { 农夫 / 夫人 }　　省 { 省力 / 省钱 }　　动 { 活动 / 劳动 }

注：*以后的字词为选做题，后同。

词语运用

忽然

① 下午三点，忽然刮起了大风。

② 我们看电视时，忽然停电了。

成功

① 不经过努力，哪能有成功。

② 哥哥长跑得了第一，他成功了！

回答问题

1. 人们为什么笑话这个等兔子的农夫？
2. 说一说，你有没有犯过"守株待兔"这样的错误？（wù）
3. 禾苗应该怎样生长才好？用不用拔高？

词语解释

守株待兔——形容不经过努力，就想得到成功。

拔苗助长——比喻只按自己的想法做事，急于求成，反而坏事。

儿 歌

农夫种禾苗，

不见禾苗长。

心里一着急，

下田拔苗苗。

禾苗被拔高，

农夫喜洋洋。

再去田里看，

禾苗全变黄。

甲骨文　金文　小篆　楷书

← 水稻

← 水田

← 禾苗

思考题

"守株待兔"和"拔苗助长"讲的都是春秋时期农夫的故事。这说明春秋时期的中国：

  A. 有许多农民，他们靠种地生活

  B. 有很多牧人，他们靠放羊生活

宋国位置示意图

Guarding the Tree Trunk to Wait for Rabbits

In the Spring-and-Autumn period, China consisted of many kingdoms. Song was a small kingdom. The peasant who worked in his fields had a hard time every day. He worked under the hot sun and got wet in the rain. One day, while he was labouring away, he saw a rabbit running full pelt across the field and bump into a tree trunk so hard that it broke its neck. The peasant picked up the rabbit and surprised his family with a rabbit stew for dinner. Then he thought: "How silly I am to labor on my fields day after day!" He gave up work and instead spent his days waiting and watching for the next rabbit to crash into the tree trunk.

He sure spared a lot of effort, but what did he gain? Do you think that more rabbits crashed into the tree? Later, this story became a chengyu for trying to succeed without making an effort.

Pulling at the Seedlings to Help Them Grow

Have you transplanted small plants? Of course you check up on your plants and of course you want to see them grow. This peasant in ancient China transplanted rice seedlings into his field. A lot of work. If only the seedlings would grow into tall green rice plants, and bear heavy ears of rice, he could enjoy fragrant fresh rice! He looked at his seedlings the next day, but they had not grown any taller. He looked again the second day, but they looked just the same. The third day he became impatient. He carefully pulled each seedling up a little bit to make them grow faster. What an awful idea that was. When he came to check his field on the fourth day, all seedlings had died.

This story became a chengyu for a failure due to too much eagerness.

第二课

画蛇添足

古时候，有个楚国①人给他的几个仆人一壶酒。可是酒少人多，怎么个喝法呢？于是大家商量好：每人在地上画一条蛇，谁画得快，画得像，谁就喝这壶酒。其中有个人画得很快，又很像，他以为这壶酒一定是他的了。这时，他见别人都没有画完，心想：我还来得及给蛇再添上几只脚啊！于是他一边抓过酒壶，一边得意洋洋地给蛇添上了几只脚。

---

① 楚国——春秋战国时期中国南方的一个诸侯(zhū hóu)国。

正在这时，另一个人也画完了，夺过酒壶说："蛇是没有脚的，你画的不是蛇。第一个画成蛇的是我，不是你！"最早画完蛇的人，因为给蛇添上了脚，反而没有喝上酒。

后来，人们就用成语"画蛇添足"比喻做了多余的事情反而不好。

生词

tiān 添	add	qí zhōng 其中	among them
chǔ 楚	Chu (name of a state; surname)	lái de jí 来得及	able to make it (in time)
pú rén 仆人	servant	dé yì yáng yáng 得意洋洋	perfectly pleased with oneself
hú 壶	vessel, pot	duó guò 夺过	snatch
jiǔ 酒	wine	fǎn ér 反而	on the contrary
shāng liang 商量	nigotiate, work sth. out	duō yú 多余	superfluous

听写

画蛇添足　楚　仆人　壶　酒　商量　其中　夺过

反而　得意洋洋　*来得及

比一比

楚 { 楚国 / 清楚 }　　壶 { 茶壶 / 暖壶 / 一壶酒 }　　添 { 添水 / 添茶 / 添饭 }

反义词

仆人——主人　　来得及——来不及

"酒"字的演变

甲骨文　　金文　　小篆　　楷体

词语运用

清楚

① 小华的作业写得又干净又清楚。

② 张老师讲课十分清楚。

③ 他是近视眼，黑板上的字看不清楚。

来得及

① 下星期五考(kǎo)地理，我现在复习还来得及。

② 电影还没有开始(shǐ)，马上进去还来得及。

反而

① 上课时他不但不听课，反而大声说话。

② 雨不但没停，反而越下越大。

③ 弟弟睡觉前不但不刷牙，反而吃糖，结果牙疼了。

阅读

掩(yǎn)耳盗(dào)铃

有一个人，想偷别人家门上的铃铛(dāng)，又怕拿的时候铃铛会响。于是他想出了一个办法：把自己的耳朵捂(wǔ)起来，再去偷那只铃铛。结果他还是被人抓住了，因为别人并(bìng)没有捂着耳朵。

The Man Who Completed His Drawing of a Snake by Adding Feet

Grown-ups have always liked wine and the old Chinese were no different. The servants in ancient Chu had only a small pot of wine to share, but they worked it out: The man who could draw the best snake would have it all! One of the guys was good at drawing and faster than the others. He was almost done and saw that all his mates were still busy. Sure that he would be the one who would get the drink, he reached out for the pot. Seeing that the others were still far from done with their drawings, he thought he still had time to add some final touches. So he added four little feet to his snake! At this moment, the fellow next to him had finished his snake and snatched the wine pot from his hand: "You cannot drink the wine. Your drawing is not a snake!" Quite right he was, too. Feeling too smart sometimes makes people do things that are quite dumb.

This chengyu stands for destroying an initially good effort by superfluous additions.

The Thief Who Covered His Ears to Steal a Bell

Bells were precious objects in the old times. If a thief could lay hands on a bell, he might make a fortune. This thief got within reach of his goal. The only trouble was: how could he make sure that the bell made no sound while he took it off and ran away with it? He carefully covered his own ears before snatching the bell. And was quite surprised when the people in the house rushed out and caught him!

This chengyu is used to describe a situation where someone is able to cheat himself but not the others.

第三课

狐假虎威

老虎非常凶猛,是动物之王,它捉到动物就吃。有一天,它捉到一只狐狸,正要吃的时候,狡猾的狐狸说:"你是不敢吃我的!你也不能吃我,因为天帝让我做动物的大王。你敢吃你的大王吗?"老虎一下糊涂了,狐狸什么时候成了动物之王了?

狐狸看老虎不信,就说:"老虎,假如你不信,我们到森林里走一走。我走在前面,你跟在后面,看看森林中的动物哪一个见了我不害怕,不逃跑!"于是狐狸神气活现地走在前面。一路

上，兔子、小鹿和其他小动物看见了狐狸和老虎，都纷纷逃跑。老虎看见了，还以为它们是真的怕狐狸呢。其实这些小动物怕的是狐狸后面的老虎。

后来，人们就用成语"狐假虎威"比喻借用别人的威风吓唬(hǔ)人。

自相矛盾

从前，有个人在街上卖兵器。他拿起一个盾对路边的人说："我的盾是世上最好的盾，没有一个矛能刺穿它。"然后他放下盾，又拿起一支矛大声喊："我的矛是世上最尖最快的矛，没有哪一个盾能挡得住它。"这时一位站在旁边的老人问他："如

果用你的矛去刺你的盾，那会怎样呢？"这个卖兵器的人脸红了，什么话也说不出来。

后来，人们就用成语"自相矛盾"比喻说话或做事前后相反。

生词

jiǎ 假	fake; make use of	máo dùn 矛盾	spear and shield; contradiction, conflict
wēi 威	power, might, authority	jiē shang 街上	in the street, on the market
xiōng měng 凶猛	fierce	bīng qì 兵器	weapon
zhī 之	of	shì shang 世上	on earth
jiǎ rú 假如	suppose, if	cì 刺	penetrate, stab
shén qì huó xiàn 神气活现	proud and self-assured	dǎng zhù 挡住	block, protect
fēn fēn 纷纷	one by one		

听写

狐假虎威　凶猛　假如　街上　兵器　自相矛盾

世上　挡住　刺　*神气活现

比一比

街 { 街上　街灯
　　街道　大街

器 { 兵器
　　机器

反义词

真——假　　狡猾——老实　　敢——怕

词语运用

假如

① 假如明天下雨，我们就不去公园了。

② 假如你不信，我们就到森林里走走。

③ 弟弟问："假如月亮上有白兔，它每天吃什么呢？"

回答问题

1. "狐假虎威"故事中，狐狸是怎样骗过老虎的？

2. 讲一讲你看到的"自相矛盾"的事情。

3. 孙悟空的兵器是什么？

　　猪八戒和沙僧呢？（看图）

西游记

词语解释

狐假虎威——比喻借别人的威风来吓唬人。

神气活现——形容十分得意的样子。

自相矛盾——比喻说话或做事前后相反。

表演剧

新东方学院秋香老师

角色：狐狸、老虎、小兔、小鹿

旁白：老虎非常凶猛，是动物之王，它捉到动物就吃。一天，它捉住了一只狐狸，正要吃……

（老虎抓着狐狸出场）

狐狸：（眼珠一转）你是不能吃我的！天帝让我做动物的大王，你敢吃你的大王吗？

老虎：（自言自语）狐狸？大王？狐狸什么时候成了大王了？

狐狸：假如你不信，我们到森林里走一走，我在前，你在后，看看哪个动物见了我不害怕，不逃跑！

（狐狸在前面走着，老虎在后面跟着。小兔、小鹿出场，看见它们马上逃跑）

小兔、小鹿：老虎来了，快跑！快跑！

旁白：其实，小动物们怕的不是狐狸，而是它后面的大老虎！以后，人们就用"狐假虎威"比喻借别人的威风来吓唬人。

 English Translation

The Fox Who Seemed as Great as the Tiger

Can a fox intimidate the tiger? This one did. At first, things looked bad for the fox, when the tiger cornered him. But the fox didn't lose his cool and calmly said to the tiger: "You cannot eat me, I'm the king of the animals." The tiger laughed in disbelief. The fox said: "I'll show you, just walk right behind me through the forest, you'll see!" The tiger could not believe his eyes: all animals of the forest ducked or ran as soon as the fox showed his nose! For a clever fox, this was a very clever fox.

This chengyu is mostly used to say that someone made himself appear important by pretending that he was connected with someone important.

As Spear and Shield

An eager salesman of weapons praised the shield for sale: "Look at this shield, you will find no better! No weapon can penetrate this shield!" Then he took out a spear. "Do you see this spear! The sharpest of all! No armour withstands this spear!" So far so good, but have you found a hitch with the saleman's logic? Do you think he sold his shield or spear?

The spear and the shield in the praise of this salesman became a chengyu for a contradiction.

第四课

滥竽充数

战国时期①,齐国②的国王喜欢听吹竽。他喜欢听很多人一起吹竽。每次表演,吹竽队都由三百人组成。

有个南郭先生跟齐王说他会吹竽,想参加吹竽队。齐王同意了,还给了他很高的工钱。

后来,齐王死了,他的儿子当了齐王。他也喜欢听吹竽,不

---

① 战国时期——中国历史上的一个时期(前475年—前221年)。
② 齐国——中国春秋战国时期的一个诸侯国(zhū hóu)。

过,他喜欢让乐手单独吹。这样一来,南郭先生没办法了,只好偷偷地逃跑了。

原来南郭先生根本不会吹竽。大家一起吹的时候,他拿着竽摇头晃脑假装在吹,却不敢吹出声音。周围的人不注意,还以为他会吹呢。可是到了单独吹的时候,他就会被人发现了。

后来,人们用成语"滥竽充数"比喻没有真正的能力,却在有能力的人里面充数。

生词

làn yú chōngshù 滥竽充数	a useless pipe that makes up the number	tōu tōu de 偷偷地	secretly
zhàn guó 战国	The Warring States period	gēn běn 根本	at all, totally
qí guó 齐国	Qi (name of a state; surname)	jiǎ zhuāng 假装	pretend
gōng qian 工钱	wage, salary	zhōu wéi 周围	surrounding
yuè shǒu 乐手	musician	zhù yì 注意	to notice
dān dú 单独	separately		

听写

滥竽充数　　战国　　工钱　　乐手　　单独　　根本　　假装

周围　　注意

比一比

逃 { 逃跑 / 逃走 }　　　　单 { 单独 / 单数 }

队 { 篮球队 / 足球队 / 网球队 }　　　　假 { 假如 / 假装 / 狐假虎威 }

多音字

乐 yuè { 音乐 / 乐手 }（yuè）　　　　乐 lè { 快乐 / 乐意 }（lè）

词语运用

滥竽充数

① 他篮球打得不好，还去比赛，这不是滥竽充数吗？

② 作业胡乱写写就交上去，这不是滥竽充数吗？

注意

① 写字时要注意身体坐正。

② 开车时要注意红绿灯。

根本

① 原来，南郭先生根本不会吹竽。

② 他一直在玩儿，根本就没听老师讲课。

词语解释

滥竽充数——比喻没有真正的能力，却在有能力的人里面充数；也形容把不好的东西放在好的里面充数。

熟能生巧

从前，有一个人射箭百发百中，观看的人都大声叫好，而一位卖油的老人只是点了点头。他问老人："我射得不好？"老人说："你射得好是好，但也没什么了不起，不过是熟练罢了。"说完，老人拿出一只葫芦放在地上，就往葫芦里倒油，只见油像一条细线流入葫芦口，一点儿都没有流到外边。观看的人大声叫好。老人说："我也不过是熟能生巧，谈不上什么高明！"

A Useless Pipe That Makes up the Number

In ancient China, the finest musical instruments were bells, zithers, and pipes. People liked music as much as they do today, and they believed that music could join our human world with the sphere of the gods, that is and was an art that transforms us and makes us more fully human. Chu was a large and powerful kingdom, and its kings were rich. Now the king of Chu liked pipe music, and he liked many pipers playing together. At his court, he maintained 300 pipers and had them all play together. Master Nanguo came to Chu, he claimed that he was a renowned piper and wanted to join the pipers' orchestra. The king welcomed him and paid him well. When the pipers were called to perform, everyone saw him diligently blowing away. Years passed. Then the old king died and his son ascended to the throne. The young king also liked pipe music, but he preferred solo pipers. Soon after the death of the old king, master Nanguo went missing and was not seen again. In fact, everyone had always seen him play, but nobody had ever heard him. Because master Nanguo could not play at all!

This chengyu describes somebody who is no good at his task but very good at blending in.

Long-time Practice Contributes to Admirable Skills

In ancient China, the art of archery was highly regarded. When an archer demonstrated his skill and hit the eye with every shot, everyone cheered and was full of admiration. Only an old oil salesman was unimpressed. When people asked him why, he said that the skill was simply long-time practice. He put a little calabash bottle on the ground and filled it by pouring oil from a large jug with a large ladle. He held the ladle high above the calabash so that the jet of poured oil was exactly thin enough when it got to the mouth of the calabash. Not a drop of oil was spilled. "Have been doing this for a long time," said the oil salesman, "that's practice."

The chengyu tells us that all skills are worth admiring and that we can only achieve it by long-time practice.

第五课

鹬(yù)蚌相争

战国时期，赵国有一次要打燕国，燕国的大臣苏代听说后急忙来到赵国，想劝赵王不要去打燕国。

苏代见了赵王，就对他说："大王，请听我给您讲一个故事：我到赵国来的时候，经过一条大河，看见一只大蚌在河滩上张开贝壳晒太阳。正在这时，一只鹬来了，伸出长嘴想去吃蚌肉。谁知道蚌马上合上了贝壳，死死地夹住鹬的长嘴。鹬不能动了，就说：'快放开我，不然今天不下雨，明天不下雨，你一定

会干死。'蚌回答说:'今天不放开你,明天不放开你,你一定会饿死。'正当鹬蚌各不相让的时候,一位渔翁跑来,把它们都捉住了。现在,如果赵国和燕国打仗,就跟鹬和蚌相争一样,而强大的秦国会像渔翁一样得利。"赵王听了苏代的话,连连点头,觉得很有道理,于是就不去打燕国了。

后来,人们就用成语"鹬蚌相争"比喻双方各不相让,第三方就会得到好处。

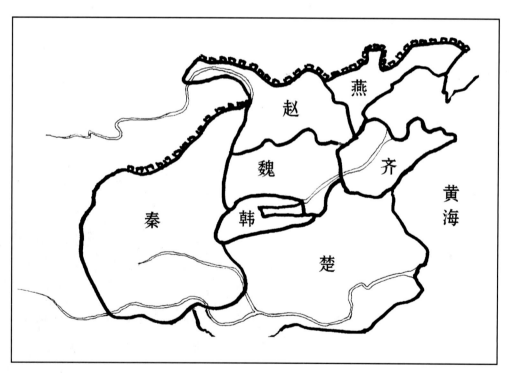

战国七雄形势图

生词

yù bàng xiāng zhēng		bèi ké	
鹬蚌相争	when the sandpiper and the clam struggle with each other	贝壳	shell
zhào		shài	
赵	Zhao (*name of a state*; *surname*)	晒	bask in the sun
dà chén		hé shang	
大臣	minister	合上	close
sū		jiā zhù	
苏	Su (*surname*)	夹住	clamp tight
quàn		yú wēng	
劝	recommend, convince	渔翁	fisherman
jīngguò		qiáng dà	
经过	pass by	强大	strong
hé tān		lì	
河滩	river bank	利	advantage

听写

赵　大臣　苏　劝　经过　河滩　晒太阳　合上

夹住　强大　渔翁得利　*贝壳

比一比

各 { 各位 / 各不相让 }　　名 { 名字 / 第一名 }

夹 { 夹住 / 夹子 }　　合 { 合起来 / 合作 }

词语运用

各

① 王老师说："各位家长、各位同学，你们好！"

② 正当鹬蚌相争、各不相让时，渔翁把它们都捉住了。

跟……一样

① 这件衣服跟那件衣服的颜色一样。

② 这辆卡车跟那辆小汽车跑得一样快。

③ 我刚十四岁，已经长得跟爸爸一样高了。

回答问题

为什么鹬和蚌会一起被渔翁捉住？

阅读

疑人偷斧（yí fǔ）

从前，有一个农夫丢了一把斧头。他想一定是邻居的孩子偷去了。于是，他看这个孩子，无论是放牛还是打草，都好像偷了他的斧头一样，躲躲闪闪的。

不久，他的斧头在自己家的院子里找到了。以后，他再看见邻居的孩子，怎么看，也看不出这个孩子像个偷东西的人。

儿歌

大河滩上一只蚌，

张开蚌壳晒太阳。

突然飞来一只鹬，

尖嘴要吃大河蚌。

河蚌夹住鹬的嘴，

双方谁也不相让。

渔翁看见真高兴，

一起抓住鹬和蚌。

When the Sandpiper and the Clam Struggle with Each Other

In the period of the Warring States, Yan and Zhao were small kingdoms squeezed between larger neighbors. To their west was the most formidable state, the kingdom of Qin. The King of Yan was told that the King of Zhao was preparing for war against his kingdom. Straightaway, the Minister of Yan went to see the King of Zhao. He told him the following story: "On my journey here, I came by a river where I saw a sandpiper with a clam clasped on its beak. I heard the sandpiper say to the clam that it would dry out and die if it did not drop back in the water for a day or two. I heard the clam say to the sandpiper that it would die of starvation if held fast for a day or two. As the two struggled, a fisherman came by and grabbed both. " The King of Zhao listened and dropped his plan of waging war on Yan. He understood that Qin was the fisherman.

This chengyu is about compromise. If two keep fighting without looking left or right, the third will win at their expense.

The Suspicion of Having Stolen the Axe

Once upon a time, a man lost his axe. He was convinced that the neighbor's boy had stolen it. The man used to watch the boy, and thought his every move was suspicious. Later, he found the axe in his own courtyard. The neighbor's boy never knew that he was suspected of having stolen an axe, nor that it turned out that he had not done it. He carried on as usual. Yet in the eyes of the man who had lost and found his axe, the boy never looked quite the same. He could not help thinking that the boy somehow looked as if he would be capable of stealing an axe.

第六课

胸有成竹

北宋时有一位著名的画家叫文同。他画的竹子远近闻名,每天都有不少人到他家来买画。

文同画竹子为什么画得好呢?原来,文同在自己家的房前屋后种上了各种各样的竹子,无论春夏秋冬,都去竹林看竹子。他看竹枝的长短粗细,看叶子的形状、颜色,然后回到书房,把竹子画在纸上。时间久了,竹子在不同季节、不同天气的样子都深深印在他的心中。他只要拿起笔,在画纸前一站,平时看到的竹

子就出现在眼前。所以每次画竹，他都画得又快又好。

当人们夸他的画时，他说："我只是把心中想了很久的竹子画了出来。"后来人们都说，文同画竹，胸中有成竹。人们也用"胸有成竹"这个成语比喻做事之前已做好了准备，对事情的成功有十分的把握。

竹文化

中国南方生长着许多竹子。自古以来，中国人的生活离不开竹子。竹笋(sǔn)好吃，竹筷好用，提竹篮，吹竹笛，放爆(bào)竹，坐竹椅，住竹楼，用竹子做的毛笔写字……现在竹子还可以做竹丝毛巾、竹地板等。我们只要打开字典，看看那些有竹字头的字，就知道竹子处处在我们的生活中。

竹子也深入到中国的文化中。竹在画中，竹在诗中，竹在成语中，竹在文章中。中国人爱竹，画竹写诗(shī)美化生活。对了，国宝大熊猫是最爱吃竹子的。

竹笋　竹篮　竹笛　筷子　爆竹　竹简　毛笔　竹席　笋

生词

xiōng yǒu chéng zhú 胸有成竹	have a well-thought-out plan	chū xiàn 出现	appear
yuǎn jìn wén míng 远近闻名	renowned far and wide	kuā 夸	praise
fáng wū 房屋	house	bǎ wò 把握	to have mastered
wú lùn 无论	whether	zhú kuài 竹筷	bamboo chopsticks
jì jié 季节	season	zhú dí 竹笛	bamboo flute
shēn shēn 深深	deeply	lóu 楼	floor of a building
yìn 印	print	zì diǎn 字典	dictionary
píng shí 平时	usually		

听写

胸有成竹　远近闻名　房屋　无论　季节　深深

平时　把握　筷子　楼　*字典

近义词

房子——屋子　　　　　　　　有把握——有信心

著名——有名——闻名

词语运用

（没）有把握

① 你有把握把他救出来吗？

② 这样做太危险了，我没有把握。

无论

① 无论你说什么，弟弟都不听。

② 无论天气好坏，哥哥都出去跑步。

回答问题

1. 人们用"胸有成竹"比喻什么？

2. 你做什么事，可以做到"胸有成竹"呢？

词语解释

远近闻名——远处和近处都很有名。

诗画欣赏

竹　石

（清）郑(zhèng)板桥

咬定青山不放松，

立根原在破岩中。

千磨万击还坚劲(jiān jìng)，

任尔(ěr)东西南北风。

书法欣赏

汉字的字体多样，有的看起来很重，像石头一样硬(yìng)，有的看起来很轻，像蝴蝶在飞。下面四幅字里，写了哪三个成语？

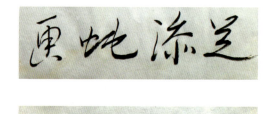

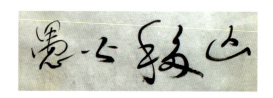

Have a Well-thought-out Plan

The Northern Song was a great period of painting. Painters depicted the changing world around them, the crowded streets of the great cities or the mills with the great wooded cog-wheels. Even more, they liked to paint nature: Flowers and butterflies for the joy of life, snowy landscapes to keep cool in summer, and rich summer scapes for comfort in winter. And they liked bamboo, the plant that will never bend under wind and rain but stand tall and proud afterwards.

Wentong was a painter who was famous for his bamboo. He maintained a bamboo garden with many different kinds of bamboo and studied the plants at different times of the year. People who saw him paint said that when he started to put a bamboo on an empty sheet, the "finished bamboo was already in his chest." They were not saying that he was growing full of bamboo inside, but that he was able to call up images of different bamboo in different settings in his mind, and then paint these.

This is a chengyu about true excellence that looks effortless, because it is the fruit of long preparation.

Bamboo Culture

Bamboo grows in many places in China, especially in the south. From ancient times, people have used bamboo for many things. They enjoy tasty bamboo sprouts, use hand bamboo chopsticks, carry bamboo baskets, play bamboo flutes, let off bamboo firecrackers, sit on bamboo chairs, live in bamboo houses, write with bamboo brushes … Nowadays bamboo is also made into towels and floors. Try to look up the character in a Chinese dictionary and see how many words contain bamboo. Bamboo is simply inseparable from our daily lives!

And it is part of Chinese culture as well. You'll find it in art, in poetry, in literature and in chengyu. Chinese love the bamboo and use it in art and poetry to make life more beautiful. And the panda loves it, too.

第七课

望梅止渴

有一年夏天,曹操带着军队去打仗。天气很热,火红的太阳当空照。士兵们在山路上行走,衣服都湿透了,越走越慢。

曹操看到士兵们走不快,心里很着急。可是,眼下几万人马连水都喝不上,怎么能走得快呢?他立刻叫来向导,小声地问:"这附近有水吗?"向导摇摇头说:"泉水在山谷的那一边,还要走很远的路。"曹操想了一下,说:"不行,时间来不及。"他看了看前边的树林,想了一会儿,对向导说:"你什么也别

说，我来想办法。"他知道这时即使下命令军队也走不快。他眼珠一转，办法来了。曹操一夹马肚子，赶到队前，指着前方说："士兵们，我知道前面有一大片梅林，那里的梅子又大又好吃。我们只要快点走，过了这座山就到梅林了！"士兵们一听，好像又大又甜的梅子就在眼前，嘴里流出了口水，也有了精神。军队马上快步前进。

后来，人们用成语"望梅止渴"比喻用空想安慰自己。

生词

wàng méi zhǐ kě 望梅止渴	the plums ahead quench the thirst	shān gǔ 山谷	valley
cáo cāo 曹操	Cao Cao (*name of a person*)	jí shǐ 即使	even if
jūn duì 军队	troops, army	mìng lìng 命令	order
dǎ zhàng 打仗	war, fight	zhuàn 转	turn
lì kè 立刻	immediately	jīng shen 精神	spirit, energy
fù jìn 附近	nearby	ān wèi 安慰	console oneself
quán shuǐ 泉水	spring water		

听写

望梅止渴　军队　打仗　立刻　附近　泉水　山谷

命令　转　*即使　安慰

比一比

止　　　正

止 { 停止 / 望梅止渴　　军 { 军队 / 军人　　命 { 命令 / 生命

反义词

大——小　　甜——苦

止字的演变

词语运用

立刻

① 红灯一亮,立刻停车!

② 他的腿受了伤,要立刻送医院。

附近

① 曹操问向导:"附近有没有水?"

② 学校就在我家附近,十分钟就能走到。

即使

① 妈妈是个热心人,即使不认识的人她也会帮助。

② 在旧金山,即使是夏天,海风也很凉。

回答问题

1. 一年夏天,曹操带领军队去干什么?

2. 士兵们为什么越走越慢?

3. 曹操用什么办法让军队走快了?

阅读

汉语中的成语

我们学中文，已学过很多种词语，比如：

- 单字词：大、小、多、少、家、树……

- 两个字组成的词：汽车、火车、飞机……

- 三个字组成的词语：来不及、不小心、另一个……

- 四个字组成的成语：守株待兔、画蛇添足……

成语多为四字组成的固定词组，有的包含着一个有哲(zhé)理的寓言或一段(duàn)生动的历史故事：如"狐假虎威"是一个寓言；"望梅止渴"就是一个历史故事。成语使汉语更简练、生动。

两千多年前的春秋战国时期就有了成语，至今成语已有几万条。成语就像菜(cài)里的盐，如果你说话、写文章用上成语，你的中文就有味道了！

选自中国集邮总公司《成语典故》特种邮票

The Plums Ahead Quench the Thirst

Cao Cao was one of the great military leaders of the Three Kingdoms. We all know that leading an army is not easy, but have we thought of what you need to do to get the army to the battlefield? Cao Cao led his troops far and wide across China, and that meant that they really had to march for a long time. Once, on a forced march across arid lands, Cao Cao saw his men sweating and the horses hanging their heads. He asked the scouts whether there was any water nearby, but he was told that the next spring was in the next valley. He knew they had to reach the valley to set up camp where water was available. But how? He told the scout not to let on that water was still far off and not to worry. Then he rode up to the front and called out: "Do you see that copse ahead? There are plums trees and the plums are ripe and juicy!" Suddenly, the tired men felt much better at the thought of having plums soon, and marched much faster. They were cheated, but they made it to the fresh water and a good camp.

As a chengyu, this story came to be used to describe a situation where we resort to illusions to comfort ourselves.

Chinese Chengyu

Most chengyu are made up of four characters. They are quite short and seem like a word. In fact, they are allusions to stories from the past and have a deep meaning about life, especially about the human mind. The fox who pretended to be a fearsome as the tiger is a fable, the story of the plum forest ahead that helped to soldiers to overcome their thirst is from ancient history. Chengyu are simple, condensed, and vivid.

From The Spring and Autumn period over 2000 years ago, chengyu have been used in China, and by today 20,000 are known! They are like salt in cooking: If you use them in telling a story or writing an essay, your Chinese gains flavour!

第八课

塞翁失马

战国时期，北方边塞住着一个老人。一天，他的一匹马跑丢了。邻居们都来劝他，年岁大了，不要着急，身体健康重要。老人笑了笑说："丢一匹马损失不大，说不定还会带来什么福气呢。"邻居们听了他的话，觉得好笑。马丢了，明明是件坏事，他却认为也许是好事。这只不过是安慰自己。

过了些日子，那匹丢了的马又跑回来了，还带回了一匹好

马。邻居们知道后，都来祝贺："真是福气呀，马不但没丢，而且还带回一匹好马。"老人听了，没有一点儿高兴的样子，反而担心地说："白白得了一匹好马，不一定是福气，也许会带来什么麻烦。"

老人的儿子喜欢骑马。他每天骑着那匹好马游玩儿。一天，他不小心从马背上摔下来，腿摔断了。邻居们都来安慰他。老人说："腿断了却保住了性命，也许是福气呢。"

不久，打仗了，青年人都去当兵，许多人死在战场。老人的儿子因为腿断了，不能打仗，保住了性命。

后来，人们用成语"塞翁失马"比喻坏事有时可以变成好事，好事也可以变成坏事。

生词

sài wēng shī mǎ 塞翁失马	Old Sai loses his horse		dān xīn 担心	worry
biān sài 边塞	frontier		má fan 麻烦	trouble
jiàn kāng 健康	health		shuāi 摔	fall
zhòng yào 重要	important		duàn 断	break
sǔn shī 损失	lose; loss		zhàn chǎng 战场	battleground
fú qi 福气	good fortune		bǎo zhù 保住	save, safeguard
zhù hè 祝贺	congratulate		xìng mìng 性命	life

听写

塞翁失马　边塞　健康　重要　损失　福气　祝贺

担心　麻烦　断　性命　*摔

反义词

担心——放心

词语运用

祝（贺）

① 祝妈妈母亲节快乐！

② 祝贺你游泳比赛得了第一名！

麻烦

① 老人心想，白白得了一匹好马，说不定会带来麻烦。

③ 爸爸一句一句地教我读课文，从来不怕麻烦。

不但……而且……

① 老人的马不但没丢，而且还带回一匹好马。

② 他不但学习好，而且喜欢养各种小动物。

回答问题

1. 为什么老人说"白白得了一匹好马，不一定是什么福气"？

2. 为什么老人的儿子摔断了腿也不一定是坏事？

3. 你有没有碰到过好事和坏事相互转变的情况？请说一说。

词语解释

塞翁失马——比喻坏事有时也可以变成好事，两者可以相互转变。

看图写故事

如何看图写故事？

1. 看dǒng懂故事内容（仔细看4张图）
2. 文章结构匀yún chèn称

   一般分三bān段：开头　中间　结尾jié（如图）

   a. 第一段　开头（参看图1）

   　　要求：开门见山　直奔主tí题　要简短

   b. 第二段　主要故事情节（参看图2和图3）

   　　要求：故事情节完整，写点细节

   c. 第三段　结尾（参看图4）

   　　要求：扣kòu题，不要太长

3. 文章字数　约250字

图1	图2
图3	图4

开头

中间

结尾

例　《塞翁失马》

1

2

3

4

提纲

第一段　开头（图1）

第二段　故事主要情节展开，细节：邻居与塞翁(zhǎn)的对话和塞翁的想法（图2和图3）

第三段　结尾，扣题：好事和坏事可以变换（图4）

文章

边塞上住着一个老人。一天，他的一匹马跑丢了。

不久，那匹马又跑回来了，还带回了一匹好马。邻居们都说："真有福气呀，马不但没丢，而且还带回一匹好马。"老人反而担心地说："白白得了一匹好马，不一定是福气，也许会带来什么麻烦。"老人的儿子喜欢骑着那匹好马游玩儿。有一天，他不小心从马背上摔下来，腿断了。老人说："腿断了却保住了性命，也许是福气呢。"

不久，打仗了，青年人都去当兵，不少人死在战场。老人的儿子因为腿断了没去打仗，保住了性命。好事和坏事是可以变换的。

Old Sai Loses His Horse

The Warring States period bears its name for a reason: The kingdoms of China were frequently at war. Old Sai lived in these times, and owned a horse. Horses were valuable because they carried goods and pulled war chariots. One day, Old Sai's horse disappeared and could not be found. His neighbors were concerned about him and tried to comfort him, but Old Sai was not upset at the loss. After some time, the horse in fact returned and brought another fine horse with it. The neighbors were happy for Old Sai, but he worried. Old Sai's young son took a horse to ride. One day he took a fall and broke his leg. The neighbors were shocked and came by to see whether they could do anything for the family, but Old Sai was calm and smiling. Not long afterwards, war broke out, and Old Sai's son was not drafted. When Old Sai lost his horse, he said something good might come from the loss. When two horses returned, he said that nothing good would come from obtaining a horse for free. When his son broke his leg he said that their might be good fortune in the accident, and in fact it saved his son's life. Old Sai was a wise old man after all.

The chengyu came to stand for the insight that good things may come out of bad luck, while bad things may come out of good luck.

第九课

伯乐①相马

春秋时期，有个叫伯乐的人，很会看马。

一次，楚王请伯乐帮忙买一匹能日行千里的马。伯乐说，千里马少有，很难找，请楚王不要着急。

伯乐跑了好几个国家，都没有发现千里马。一天，伯乐在路上看到一匹马拉着车，吃力地往山上走，只见马累得呼呼喘气。可是，马见到伯乐，突然大声嘶叫。伯乐从叫声中听出这是一匹难得的好马。

伯乐对赶车人说："这匹马如果在战场上飞奔，任何马都比不过它，但是用来拉车，却不如普通的马。你还是把它卖给我吧。"赶车人觉得伯乐是个大傻瓜。他看这匹马太普通了，拉车没力气，吃得又多，于是二话没说就同意了。

伯乐带着马去见楚王。楚王仔细一看，马瘦得不成样子，有

---

① 伯乐——传说中，天上管理马匹的神仙叫伯乐。在人间，人们把会看马的人也称为伯乐。

点儿不高兴,说:"我相信你会看马,可是你买的是什么马呀,连走路都困难,能上战场吗?"伯乐说:"这确实是匹千里马,由于让它拉车,又没有好好儿喂它,所以很瘦。只要用心喂养,过一段时间,它就会强壮起来的。"

楚王听了,半信半疑,只好让马夫用心喂养。果然没多久,这匹马就变得十分强壮。楚王骑着它奔跑,只觉得两耳生风,一会儿就跑出百里之外。以后,楚王骑着这匹千里马打了很多胜仗。

后来,人们就用成语"伯乐相马"比喻会发现人才。

生词

bó lè 伯乐	Bole (name of a person)	yóu yú 由于	for the reason that period (of time);
chuǎn qì 喘气	out of breath	duàn 段	*measure word*
fēi bēn 飞奔	run at top speed	qiáng zhuàng 强壮	strong
rèn hé 任何	any	bàn xìn bàn yí 半信半疑	be half-believing and half-doubting
pǔ tōng 普通	common, ordinary	guǒ rán 果然	in the end
zǐ xì 仔细	carefully, meticulously	shèng 胜	win; victorious
què shí 确实	in fact		

听写

伯乐相马　任何　普通　仔细　确实　由于　段

强壮　果然　胜　*喘气　飞奔

比一比

奔 { 飞奔 / 奔跑　　吃 { 吃力 / 吃饭　　通 { 普通 / 通过

近义词

仔细——认真　　　由于——因为

强壮——健壮　　　粗心大意——马马虎虎

反义词

仔细——粗心　　　相信——怀疑

多音字

lěi
累

累(lěi)：累积、日积月累

lèi
累

累(lèi)：劳累、累坏了

量词

一段时间　　一段公路

一段课文　　一段故事

一段木头　　一段铁路

词语运用

仔细

① 你仔细想一想,东西到底放在哪儿了?

② 小华画画很仔细,一幅画画了三个小时。

③ 他把这封信仔细地看了一遍。

由于

① 由于天气不好,飞机不能起飞。

② 由于每天游泳,姐姐全身晒得黑黑的。

③ 由于爱吃糖,弟弟的牙都坏了。

果然

① 果然没多久,这匹马就强壮起来。

② 弟弟不洗手就吃东西,果然生病了。

③ 我觉得这次足球比赛法国队会赢,果然法国队后来赢了。

Bole, the Horse Whisperer

In ancient China horses were the symbol of speed and power, bred by the mighty kings. Bole was a man who could tell the quality of a horse just by looking at it. His skill was considered great.

The King of Chu ordered him to find a horse that could run a thousand Li in a single day. Bole searched for many years in many kingdoms, but found no horse could perform the feat of running 1,000 Li in a day. At long last, he passed a bony old horse that slowly pulled a cart up a small hill. He looked it over and the horse called out to him. He asked the man what horse he had there, and was told that the beast was just about useless. It ate a lot yet was almost too weak to pull a cart. Bole bought the horse off the man, who was happy to sell it, and returned to Chu.

The King of Chu was not pleased to see the tired animal that was so thin and could count the ribs. But Bole said it was an extraordinary war horse, brought down by being used for pulling carts. With the right care, it would recover. Fed and rested, the horse indeed was hard to recognize. It became a famous battle horse of the king and brought him good fortune.

The chengyu of Bole refers to the ability to discover not only horses that can run a thousand li, but also persons of great talent.

第十课

愚公移山

很久以前,有一位老人叫愚公,他家门口有两座大山,一座叫太行山,一座叫王屋山。两座山挡住了家门口的路,愚公出入很不方便。

一天,愚公和家人商量:"咱们全家动手,把两座大山移开,门口的路就可以通到大路了,你们说好不好?"愚公的儿子和孙子们一听,都高兴地说:"好呀!好呀!"可愚公的妻子却

摇摇头说:"你连搬一座小山的力气都没有,还想搬走大山!还有,挖出来的土和石头怎么办?"愚公和孩子们听了哈哈大笑起来,说:"我们可以把它们扔到海里去呀!"

第二天,愚公和儿孙们开始挖山。愚公的邻居是一个妇女,她带着小儿子高高兴兴地帮愚公一起移山。这时,一位叫智叟的老先生看见了,忍不住嘲笑他们说:"愚公呀!你太糊涂了。你这么老了还要移山?就算挖到你死掉的那一天,也不可能把山移走的!"

愚公听了笑笑说:"智叟,你的想法太死板了,我看你连妇女和孩子都不如。我虽然很老,可是我还有儿子、孙子,这样子子孙孙一直挖下去,山只会越挖越小,总有一天会挖掉的。"智叟听了,说不出话来,只好走了。

从此,愚公带领大家挖山不止。天帝被愚公的顽强精神感动了,就派两个天神把太行山、王屋山背走了。

后来,人们用成语"愚公移山"比喻做事情不怕困难,一直做到底的精神。

生词

愚公移山 yú gōng yí shān	Master Yu moves the mountains	忍不住 rěn bu zhù	unable to hold on
方便 fāngbiàn	convenient	嘲笑 cháo xiào	ridicule
咱们 zánmen	we	死板 sǐ bǎn	dumb
妇女 fù nǚ	woman	顽强 wán qiáng	indomitable
智叟 zhì sǒu	Zhisou (*the wise old man*)	派 pài	send, appoint
忍 rěn	bear		

听写

愚公移山　方便　咱们　妇女　忍不住　嘲笑　派　*顽强

近义词

嘲笑——笑话　　性命——生命　　妇女——女人

反义词

弱小——强大　　底下——上面

成功——失败 bài　　愚——智

多音字

biàn
便

bià n
便 { 方便　便当
　　　轻便　便饭
　　　便于　便条

pián
便

pián
便 { 便宜

词语运用

商量

① 这件事应该怎么办，你们好好儿商量一下。

② 跟爸爸妈妈意见不同的时候，不要争吵，要与他们好好儿商量。

感动

① 愚公挖山不止的精神感动了天帝。

② 他的话深深地感动了我。

只好

① 齐王让乐手单独吹竽，南郭先生只好逃走了。

② 由于外面下大雨，我们只好在家里做游戏了。

词语解释

嘲笑——笑话别人。

华夏大地上的愚公

"愚公移山"的故事写于2,000多年前的战国时期,它不是一个人的故事,它代表着华夏民族的精神:勤劳勇敢,坚定不移。千百年来,华夏民族在求生存的过程中,勇敢面对自然灾害与困难,坚持抗争。

《愚公移山》(局部)　徐悲鸿　画

- 4,000年前,相传大禹带领华夏先民开凿禹门,黄河东流入海。
- 2,500年前,修建了著名的水利工程"都江堰"。
- 1,700年前,修建世界上最长的大运河——京杭大运河(1,797千米)。
- 1940年(抗日战争时期),徐悲鸿画《愚公移山》表达中国人抗战到底的决心。

黄河禹门

相传4,000年前大禹带领人们把山凿开一个38米宽的口子（*禹门），让黄河能东流入海。禹门又叫龙门。

都江堰水利工程在四川成都，是春秋时期秦国的李冰主持修建的。那时没有铁(tiě)器，人们用火烧(shāo)山石，再泼水使石头裂开的办法开山。整整七年，人们在山上凿开一个口子（宝瓶口），使水流入成都平原。

都江堰

当代愚公

云南有八位普通的农村(cūn)老人，自1980年起，坚持在荒(huāng)山上种树。30多年，他们种树13.6万亩(mǔ)，被称为"当代愚公"。

---

* 郦(lì)道元《水经注》："龙门为禹所凿，广80步，岩际镌迹(juān jì)尚存。"

Master Yu Moves the Mountains

Master Yu was also known as Silly old man. He and his family lived between two mountains, the Taihang and the Wangwu mountains. The mountains had always been there. But Old Yu eventually got annoyed about them: "If the mountains were not in our way, we could go out from our front door right out onto the great road into the wide world. I am tired of being locked in by mountains!" His sons and grandsons agreed that the mountains were an inconvenience and something should be done about them. They started digging. The neighbors also joined in. One of the neigbors was called Wise old man, his wife and children helped digging, but he laughed at Master Yu: "How can you imagine at your age that you can remove mountains?" Master Yu brushed it off: "I am old, but I have sons and daughters, who have sons and daughters, and these will have sons and daughters. if they all continue digging, one day the mountain will be gone!" Wise old man had nothing to say at this. For a long time, Master Yu, his family, and all who wanted to join continued digging. Eventually, the Heavenly Lord noticed the little crowd labouring at the great mountains and was moved by their spirit. He sent out his genies to carry the mountains away.

The chengyu of Master Yu evokes the spirit of never giving up, no matter what the odds are.

Yugong and the Spirit of the Chinese People

The story of Yugong dates to the Warring States period, over 2000 years ago. It appears to be the story of old man Yu, in fact it captures the spirit of the Chinese people: diligence and a dedication never to give up.

There are several examples of this spirit in Chinese history:

4000 years ago, the legendary Great Yu made the Yellow River flow eastwards into the sea. He is said to have cut a 38 metres wide opening into sheer rock, the Yu Gate, which is also called the Dragon Gate.

2500 years ago, the Dujiang Weir was built. Li Bing, a minister of the State of Qin, is regarded as the builder. Cutting the diversion of the Min River took seven years and was accomplished by setting fire to the rock to make it brittle. To this day, the weir irrigates the Chengdu Plain.

1700 years ago, the Grand Canal was built.

In 1940, when the Anti-Japanese war ravaged China, Xu Beihong painted old Yu to express his conviction that the Chinese people would persevere and remain victorious.

In the 1980s eight elderly peasants in Yunnan began planting trees. In some 30 years, they have re-afforested 13.6 Mu of barren mountain slopes. They are called the "modern old Yus."

生字表（简）

1. 守(shǒu) 株(zhū) 待(dài) 宋(sòng) 忽(hū) 撞(zhuàng) 省(shěng) 喻(yù) 功(gōng) 拔(bá) 更(gèng)
2. 添(tiān) 楚(chǔ) 仆(pú) 壶(hú) 酒(jiǔ) 商(shāng) 及(jí) 洋(yáng) 夺(duó) 而(ér) 余(yú)
3. 假(jiǎ) 威(wēi) 凶(xiōng) 猛(měng) 之(zhī) 纷(fēn) 矛(máo) 盾(dùn) 街(jiē) 兵(bīng) 器(qì) 世(shì) 刺(cì) 挡(dǎng)
4. 滥(làn) 竽(yú) 充(chōng) 战(zhàn) 齐(qí) 独(dú) 根(gēn) 周(zhōu) 注(zhù)
5. 蚌(bàng) 争(zhēng) 赵(zhào) 臣(chén) 苏(sū) 劝(quàn) 滩(tān) 晒(shài) 夹(jiā) 渔(yú) 翁(wēng) 强(qiáng) 利(lì)
6. 胸(xiōng) 近(jìn) 屋(wū) 论(lùn) 深(shēn) 夸(kuā) 握(wò) 筷(kuài) 笛(dí) 楼(lóu) 典(diǎn)
7. 梅(méi) 曹(cáo) 刻(kè) 附(fù) 谷(gǔ) 即(jí) 使(shǐ) 令(lìng) 转(zhuàn) 精(jīng) 慰(wèi)
8. 塞(sài) 失(shī) 健(jiàn) 康(kāng) 损(sǔn) 失(shī) 福(fú) 贺(hè) 担(dān) 烦(fán) 摔(shuāi) 保(bǎo) 性(xìng)
9. 喘(chuǎn) 奔(bēn) 任(rèn) 普(pǔ) 仔(zǐ) 段(duàn) 疑(yí) 胜(shèng)
10. 愚(yú) 移(yí) 咱(zán) 妇(fù) 智(zhì) 叟(sǒu) 忍(rěn) 嘲(cháo) 顽(wán) 派(pài)

共计111个生字，累计1142个生字

生字表（繁）

1. 守(shǒu) 株(zhū) 待(dài) 宋(sòng) 忽(hū) 撞(zhuàng) 省(shěng) 喻(yù) 功(gōng) 拔(bá) 更(gèng)
2. 添(tiān) 楚(chǔ) 僕(pú) 壺(hú) 酒(jiǔ) 商(shāng) 及(jí) 洋(yáng) 奪(duó) 而(ér) 餘(yú)
3. 假(jiǎ) 威(wēi) 凶(xiōng) 猛(měng) 之(zhī) 紛(fēn) 矛(máo) 盾(dùn) 街(jiē) 兵(bīng) 器(qì) 世(shì) 刺(cì) 擋(dǎng)
4. 濫(làn) 竽(yú) 充(chōng) 戰(zhàn) 齊(qí) 獨(dú) 根(gēn) 周(zhōu) 注(zhù)
5. 蚌(bàng) 爭(zhēng) 趙(zhào) 臣(chén) 蘇(sū) 勸(quàn) 灘(tān) 曬(shài) 夾(jiā) 漁(yú) 翁(wēng) 強(qiáng) 利(lì)
6. 胸(xiōng) 近(jìn) 屋(wū) 論(lùn) 深(shēn) 誇(kuā) 握(wò) 筷(kuài) 笛(dí) 樓(lóu) 典(diǎn)
7. 梅(méi) 曹(cáo) 刻(kè) 附(fù) 谷(gǔ) 即(jí) 使(shǐ) 令(lìng) 轉(zhuǎn) 精(jīng) 慰(wèi)
8. 塞(sài) 失(shī) 健(jiàn) 康(kāng) 損(sǔn) 失(shī) 福(fú) 賀(hè) 擔(dān) 煩(fán) 摔(shuāi) 保(bǎo) 性(xìng)
9. 喘(chuǎn) 奔(bēn) 任(rèn) 普(pǔ) 仔(zǐ) 段(duàn) 疑(yí) 勝(shèng)
10. 愚(yú) 移(yí) 咱(zán) 婦(fù) 智(zhì) 叟(sǒu) 忍(rěn) 嘲(cháo) 頑(wán) 派(pài)

共計111個生字，纍計1142個生字

生词表（简）

1. 守株待兔 时期 宋 农夫 劳动 忽然 撞 省力
   笑话 成语 比喻 成功 拔苗助长 更

2. 添 楚 仆人 壶 酒 商量 其中 来得及 得意洋洋
   夺过 反而 多余

3. 假 威 凶猛 之 假如 神气活现 纷纷 矛盾
   街上 兵器 世上 刺 挡住

4. 滥竽充数 战国 齐国 工钱 乐手 单独 偷偷地
   根本 假装 周围 注意

5. 鹬蚌相争 赵 大臣 苏 劝 经过 河滩 贝壳
   晒 合上 夹住 渔翁 强大 利

6. 胸有成竹 远近闻名 房屋 无论 季节 深深
   印 平时 出现 夸 把握 竹筷 竹笛 楼 字典

7. 望梅止渴 曹操 军队 打仗 立刻 附近 泉水

生词表(简)

| | shān gǔ | jí shǐ | mìng lìng | zhuàn | jīng shen | ān wèi |
| | 山谷 | 即使 | 命令 | 转 | 精神 | 安慰 |

8. 塞翁失马 边塞 健康 重要 损失 福气 祝贺
(sài wēng shī mǎ biān sài jiàn kāng zhòng yào sǔn shī fú qi zhù hè)

担心 麻烦 摔 断 战场 保住 性命
(dān xīn má fan shuāi duàn zhàn chǎng bǎo zhù xìng mìng)

9. 伯乐 喘气 飞奔 任何 普通 仔细 确实 由于
(bó lè chuǎn qì fēi bēn rèn hé pǔ tōng zǐ xì què shí yóu yú)

段 强壮 半信半疑 果然 胜
(duàn qiáng zhuàng bàn xìn bàn yí guǒ rán shèng)

10. 愚公移山 方便 咱们 妇女 智叟 忍 忍不住
(yú gōng yí shān fāng biàn zán men fù nǚ zhì sǒu rěn rěn bu zhù)

嘲笑 死板 顽强 派
(cháo xiào sǐ bǎn wán qiáng pài)

共计130个生词

生词表（繁）

1. 守株待兔 時期 宋 農夫 勞動 忽然 撞 省力
   笑話 成語 比喻 成功 拔苗助長 更

2. 添 楚 僕人 壺 酒 商量 其中 來得及 得意洋洋
   奪過 反而 多餘

3. 假 威 凶猛 之 假如 神氣活現 紛紛 矛盾
   街上 兵器 世上 刺 擋住

4. 濫竽充數 戰國 齊國 工錢 樂手 單獨 偷偷地
   根本 假裝 周圍 注意

5. 鷸蚌相爭 趙 大臣 蘇 勸 經過 河灘 貝殼
   曬 合上 夾住 漁翁 強大 利

6. 胸有成竹 遠近聞名 房屋 無論 季節 深深
   印 平時 出現 誇 把握 竹筷 竹笛 樓 字典

7. 望梅止渴 曹操 軍隊 打仗 立刻 附近 泉水

生词表(繁)

	shān gǔ	jí shǐ	mìng lìng	zhuàn	jīng shen	ān wèi
	山谷	即使	命令	轉	精神	安慰

8. 塞翁失馬 邊塞 健康 重要 損失 福氣 祝賀
   （sài wēng shī mǎ　biān sài　jiàn kāng　zhòng yào　sǔn shī　fú qi　zhù hè）

擔心 麻煩 摔 斷 戰場 保住 性命
（dān xīn　má fan　shuāi　duàn　zhàn chǎng　bǎo zhù　xìng mìng）

9. 伯樂 喘氣 飛奔 任何 普通 仔細 確實 由於
   （bó lè　chuǎn qì　fēi bēn　rèn hé　pǔ tōng　zǐ xì　què shí　yóu yú）

段 強壯 半信半疑 果然 勝
（duàn　qiáng zhuàng　bàn xìn bàn yí　guǒ rán　shèng）

10. 愚公移山 方便 咱們 婦女 智叟 忍 忍不住
    （yú gōng yí shān　fāng biàn　zán men　fù nǚ　zhì sǒu　rěn　rěn bu zhù）

嘲笑 死板 頑強 派
（cháo xiào　sǐ bǎn　wán qiáng　pài）

共計130個生詞

附录

"新双双中文教材"写作练习（1—6册）

课文正式教授写作内容

内容	出处	建议学习年级
1. 课文缩写	第4册 《猴子捞月亮》	3—4年级
2. 日记	第5册 《妈妈教我写日记》	4—5年级
3. 叙事文	第5册 《参观兵马俑》	4—5年级
4. 看图写故事	第6册 成语故事《塞翁失马》	5—6年级

辅助写作练习

内容	出处	建议学习年级
1. 读书笔记	亲子阅读，每周家庭读书、写作	2—6年级
2. 观察记录	第4册 写《养蚕报告》	3—4年级
3. 创作	写简单的故事和想法	4年级以上

手工作业

石雪丽　设计

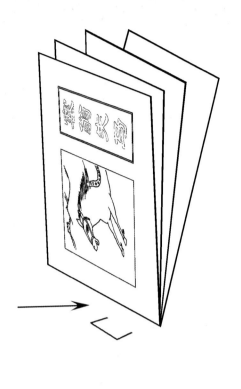

2. 再对折一次

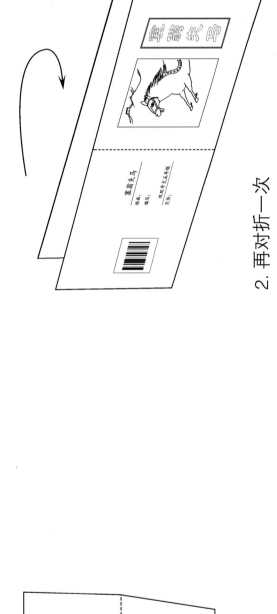

1. 沿虚线对折

4. 用钉书机钉好就成了一本书的样子

3. 用小刀划开

望梅止渴

绘画：
编写：

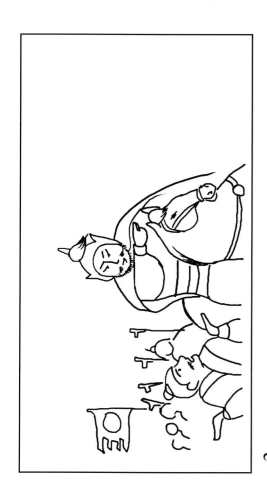

3.

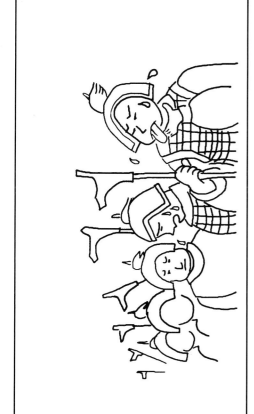

2.

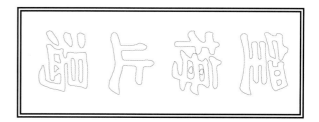

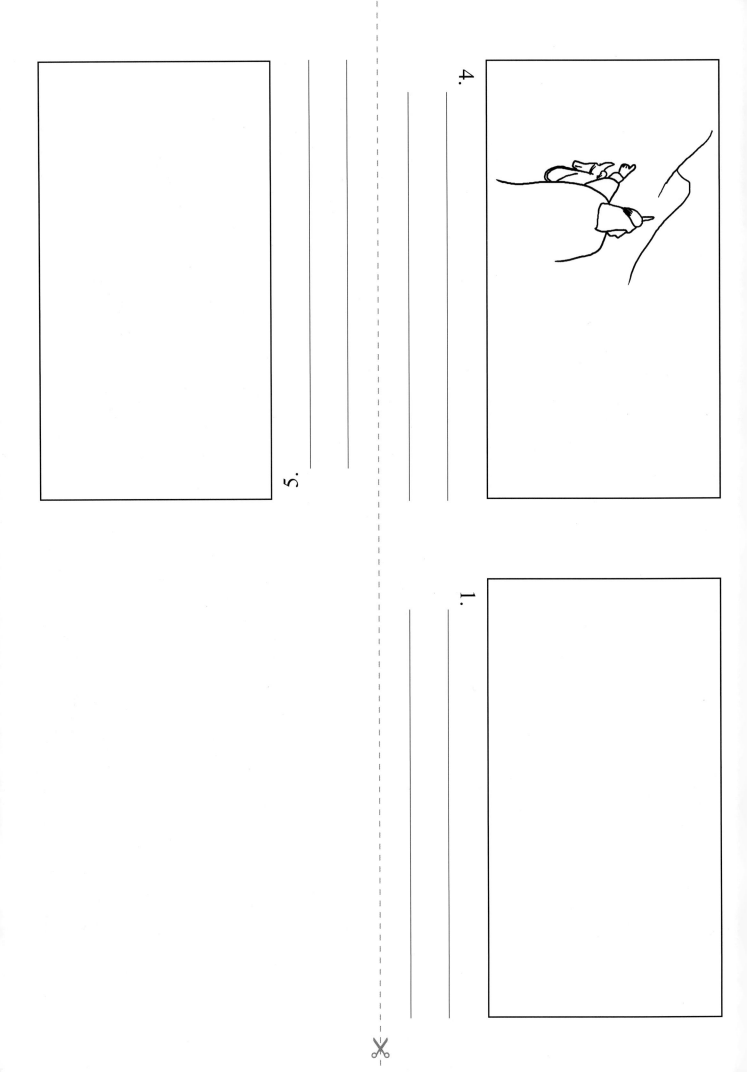

塞翁失马

绘画：
编写：

塞翁失马

2.

3.

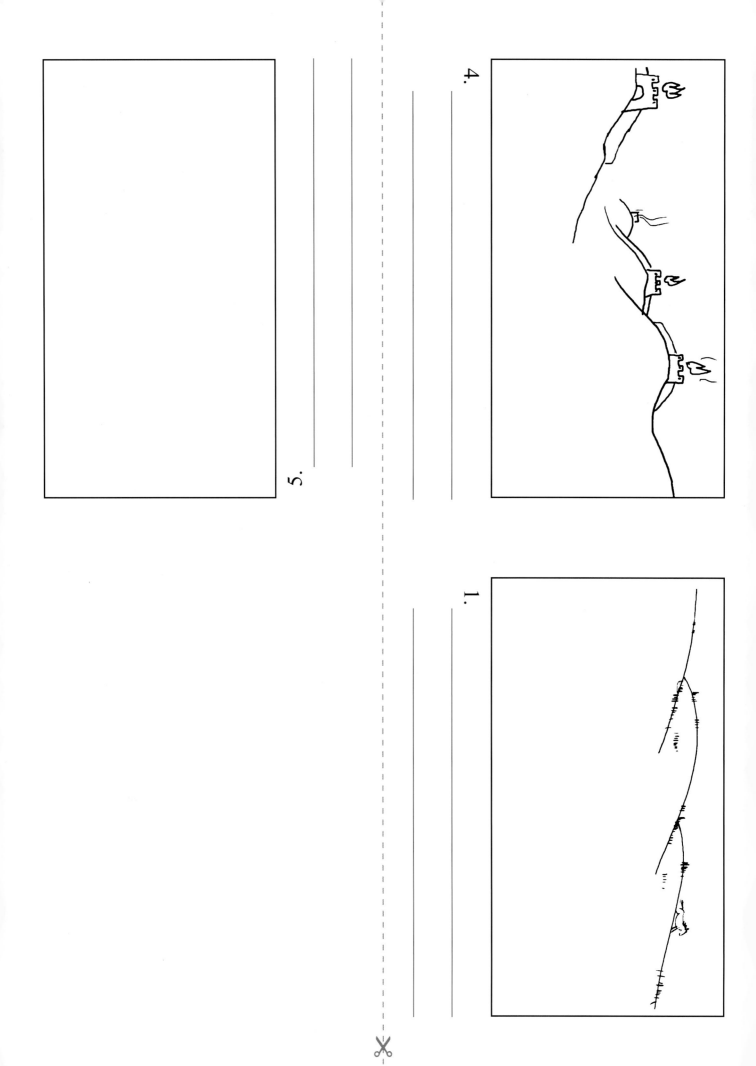

新双双中文教材 6

New Chinese Language and Culture Course

中国成语故事 Chinese Idiom Stories

练习本 单课

王双双 编著

北京大学出版社
PEKING UNIVERSITY PRESS

目 录

第一课　守株待兔　拔苗助长 ……………………………… 1

第三课　狐假虎威　自相矛盾 ……………………………… 6

第五课　鹬蚌相争 …………………………………………… 11

第七课　望梅止渴 …………………………………………… 16

第九课　伯乐相马 …………………………………………… 20

第一课
守株待兔 拔苗助长

练习一   练习二   练习三

一 写生词

宋					
撞					
更					
时	期				
农	夫				
劳	动				

忽	然				
省	力				
笑	话				
成	语				
守	株	待	兔		

二 组词

劳_____   然_____   省_____   功_____

三 下列汉字是由哪几部分组成的

省→（少）+（目）   功→（ ）+（ ）

动→（ ）+（ ）   株→（ ）+（ ）

四 选字组词

农（夫 天）   野（早 草）   （于 干）活

劳（云 动）   笑（活 话）   苹（棵 果）

第一课
守株待兔 拔苗助长

练习一　★ 练习二　☆ 练习三

一　写生词

比	喻

成	功

拔	苗	助	长

二　你在"撞"字中，能看出几个字？

☐ ☐ ☐ ☐ ☐
1　2　3　4　5

三　解释成语"守株待兔"里的每个字

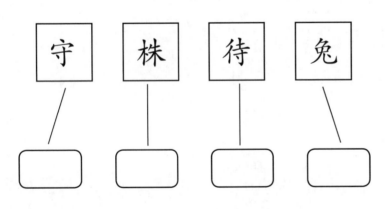

兔子	等着
树	看守

第一课 守株待兔 拔苗助长

练习一　　练习二　　练习三

四 选词填空

1. 飞跑的兔子撞到一_____大树上。（课　棵）

2. 那个农夫坐在树下_____兔子跑来。（等待　等等）

3. 那个农夫不喜欢_____。（于是　干活）

4. 人们都笑话这个_____。（农夫　丈夫）

五 根据课文判断对错

1. "守株待兔"的故事发生在春秋时期。　　___对___错

2. 兔子不小心撞到大树上死了。　　　　　___对___错

3. 农夫在树下等着，兔子就跑来了。　　　___对___错

4. 难得碰上的好事，不是天天都有。　　　___对___错

5. 农夫想让禾苗长高，就把禾苗都拔高了。___对___错

6. 禾苗可以自己长高，不能拔高。　　　　___对___错

第一课
守株待兔 拔苗助长

练习一　　练习二　　**练习三**

一　根据《拔苗助长》选择填空

1. 春秋时期，有个农夫，种了一片_____。

   　　A. 树林　　　　B. 禾苗　　　　C. 草地

2. 第二天他见禾苗没有长高，心里有点_____。

   　　A. 高兴　　　　B. 生气　　　　C. 着急

3. 于是，他把禾苗_____地都拔高了一点。

   　　A. 一棵一棵　　B. 一个一个　　C. 一支一支

二　造句

忽然_____

三　看图涂色，并写出成语故事

守　株　待　兔

第一课
守株待兔 拔苗助长

练习一　　　　练习二　　　　**练习三**

_____

_____

_____

_____

四　学了成语"守株待兔"后想一想

　　英文中有没有相同意思的话？怎么说？请写出来。

_____

五　讲一讲你生活中有没有"拔苗助长"的事情发生

六　读课文两遍，再把成语"守株待兔"和"拔苗助长"
　　讲给家人听

第三课
狐假虎威　自相矛盾

练习一　　练习二　　练习三

一　写生词

假					
威					
之					
刺					
凶	猛				
假	如				
纷	纷				

矛	盾				
街	上				
兵	器				
世	上				
挡	住				
神	气	活	现		

二　每字组两词

假	真假
	狐假虎威

街	

器	

三　选字组词

兵（哭　器）　　矛（盾　自）　　（神　伸）仙

大（哭　器）　　各（盾　自）　　（神　伸）手

第三课 狐假虎威 自相矛盾

练习一　　练习二　　练习三

四　写出反义词

老实　假　怕

真—— 　　　狡猾—— 　　　敢——

五　选词填空

1. 姐姐画的猫好极了，像_____的一样。（真 假）

2. _____的狐狸把老虎都骗了。（狡猾 老实）

3. 小动物都_____老虎。（怕 敢）

4. 天黑了，哥哥也_____一个人出去。（怕 敢）

第三课
狐假虎威 自相矛盾

练习一　**练习二**　练习三

一　在方框里找出4个成语，圈出并写在空格里

守	自	画	蛇	添	足
株	足	相	自	株	矛
待	画	添	矛	假	守
兔	狐	假	虎	盾	兔
威	狐	假	虎	威	兔

二　解释成语"狐假虎威"里每个字的意思

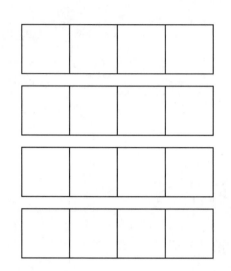

狐　假　虎　威

（借着　狐狸　威风　老虎）

三　连一连

拔苗助长　　　借用别人的威风来吓唬人

画蛇添足　　　急于求成，反而坏事

狐假虎威　　　说话或做事前后相反

自相矛盾　　　做了多余的事反而不好

第三课
狐假虎威 自相矛盾

练习一　　练习二　　练习三

四　根据课文选择填空

1. 一天，老虎捉到了_____狐狸。

    A. 一头　　　B. 一张　　　C. 一只　　　D. 一本

2. 狐狸说："假如你不信，我们到_____走走。"

    A. 院子里　　B. 花园　　　C. 森林里　　D. 草地上

3. 小动物怕的是狐狸_____的老虎。

    A. 前面　　　B. 上面　　　C. 左面　　　D. 后面

4. 有个人在_____卖兵器。

    A. 街灯　　　B. 街上　　　C. 树上

5. 卖兵器的人说："我的矛是世上_____矛。"

    A. 最美的　　B. 最亮的　　C. 最尖最快的

6. 一位站在旁边听他叫卖的_____问他一个问题。

    A. 将军　　　B. 老人　　　C. 卫士

7. 这位卖兵器的人脸_____了。

    A. 黄　　　　B. 红　　　　C. 绿

第三课
狐假虎威 自相矛盾

练习一　　练习二　　**练习三**

一　造句

其实＿＿＿＿＿＿＿＿＿＿＿＿＿＿＿＿＿＿＿＿＿＿＿

假如＿＿＿＿＿＿＿＿＿＿＿＿＿＿＿＿＿＿＿＿＿＿＿

二　请把"对牛弹琴"的故事读给家人听

对牛弹琴

从前有一个人，他弹琴弹得非常好。一天，他看见一头牛正在河边吃草，就对着牛弹了一首好听的曲子。可是牛还是低头吃草，并不理他。他生气了。放牛的人来了，说："您琴弹得非常好，只是牛听不懂。"

后来，人们用"对牛弹琴"比喻说话不看对象，等于白说。

三　朗读课文两遍

第五课 鹬蚌相争

练习一 练习二 练习三

一 写生词

赵					
苏					
劝					
晒					
利					
经	过				

河	滩				
贝	壳				
合	上				
渔	翁				
鹬	蚌	相	争		

二 组字

日 + 西 — 晒 　　　公 + 羽 — ☐

禾 + 刂 — ☐ 　　　人 + 一 + 口 — ☐

三 组词

_____ 字　　　_____ 太阳　　　_____ 边

_____ 是　　　_____ 不相让　　　_____ 死

第五课 鹬蚌相争

练习一　练习二　练习三

一　写生词

大	臣

夹	住

强	大

二　看战国地图，找出燕国、赵国和秦国，并涂上不同的颜色

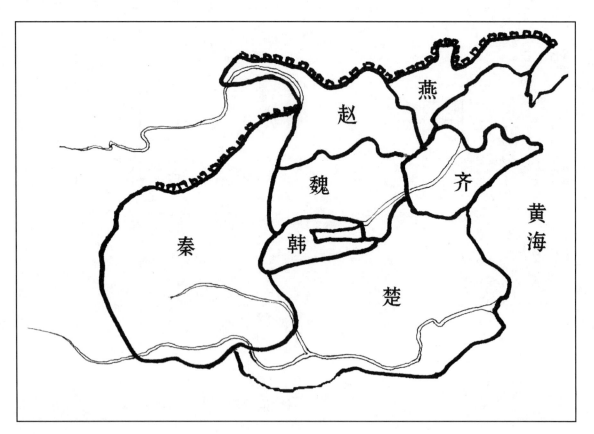

战国七雄形势图

第五课
鹬蚌相争

练习一 **练习二** 练习三

三 根据课文判断对错

1. "鹬蚌相争，渔翁得利"是一个成语。　　　___对___错

2. 燕国大臣苏代劝说赵王不要去打燕国。　　___对___错

3. 赵王听了苏代的话，不去打燕国了。　　　___对___错

4. 赵王一点儿都不糊涂。　　　　　　　　　___对___错

四 造句

跟……一样_____

各不相让_____

五 根据课文选择填空

1. 苏代给赵王讲了一个"鹬蚌相争"的_____。

　　A. 诗歌　　　　　B. 故事　　　　　C. 电影

2. 蚌张开_____晒太阳。

　　A. 长腿　　　　　B. 尖嘴　　　　　C. 贝壳

3. 课文里的"鹬蚌"指的是哪两个国家？_____

　　A. 秦国和燕国　　B. 秦国和赵国　　C. 赵国和燕国

第五课 鹬蚌相争

练习三

一 根据课文写出鹬蚌相争时的对话

二 缩写课文《鹬蚌相争》，并运用词语"各不相让"

_____
_____
_____
_____
_____
_____

第五课 鹬蚌相争

练习一　　练习二　　**练习三**

三　选字写出2个成语，多余的一个字写在方格中

争　相　利　鱼　数　渔　蚌
得　滥　翁　竽　鹬　充

1. _____
2. _____

四　根据阅读课文选词填空

1. 从前，有一个人丢了一_____斧子。（条　朵　把）

2. 他想一定是邻居家的孩子_____去了。（借　拿　偷）

3. 不久，他的斧头在自己家的院子里_____到了。

（找　捡）

五　读课文两遍

第七课 望梅止渴

练习一　　　练习二　　　练习三

一　写生词

曹	操				
军	队				
打	仗				
立	刻				
泉	水				

山	谷				
即	使				
命	令				
望	梅	止	渴		

二　组字

白 + 水 — ☐　　　　八 + 人 + 口 — ☐

木 + 每 — ☐　　　　米 + 青 — ☐

三　将下列词语分类

　　士兵　　泉水　　山谷　　带领　　梅林

　　立刻　　曹操　　向导　　命令　　不久

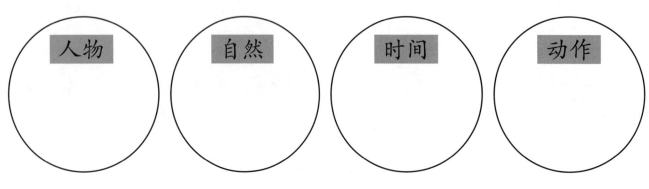

16

第七课 望梅止渴

练习一　练习二　练习三

一 写生词

| 转 | | | 附 近 | | | 精 神 | | | 安 慰 | |

二 组词

渴_____　令_____　精_____　刻_____

喝_____　今_____　请_____　孩_____

三 根据课文选择填空

1. 曹操带领_____去打仗。

　　A. 海军　　　　B. 空军　　　　C. 军队

2. 士兵们的衣服都_____了。

　　A. 潮湿　　　　B. 湿透　　　　C. 美丽

3. 向导说泉水在_____的那一边。

　　A. 河岸　　　　B. 树林　　　　C. 山谷

第七课
望梅止渴

练习一　**练习二**　练习三

4. 梅子又大又_____。

　　A. 苦　　　　B. 甜　　　　C. 咸

四　根据课文判断对错

1. 曹操带领军队去打仗,天气很冷。　　　___对___错

2. 到了晚上,曹操的军队走不快了。　　　___对___错

3. 后来,曹操知道附近没有泉水。　　　　___对___错

4. 曹操眼珠一转,办法来了。　　　　　　___对___错

5. 大家吃到了梅子。　　　　　　　　　　___对___错

6. 成语"望梅止渴",就是一个历史故事。___对___错

五　造句

即使_____

立刻_____

六　读课文两遍

第七课 望梅止渴

练习一　　练习二　　**练习三**

一　将下列词语归类

> 望梅止渴　没关系　高　哭　玩具　拿　看电影
> 欢迎　水　自相矛盾　飞机场　门　墙　大学

单字词＿＿＿＿＿＿＿＿＿＿＿＿＿＿＿＿＿＿＿＿

两个字组成的词＿＿＿＿＿＿＿＿＿＿＿＿＿＿＿＿

三个字组成的词语＿＿＿＿＿＿＿＿＿＿＿＿＿＿＿

成语＿＿＿＿＿＿＿＿＿＿＿＿＿＿＿＿＿＿＿＿＿

二　完成手工作业：自制成语小人书《望梅止渴》

要求：1. 画图并给图上色

2. 写出图画内容

3. 订成书保留

三　有趣的京剧脸谱（选做）

曹操在京剧中的脸谱是白脸。请画一张曹操的脸谱。这张脸谱给你的印象是什么？

曹操京剧脸谱

第九课
伯乐相马

★ 练习一　　☆ 练习二　　☆ 练习三

一　写生词

段					
胜					
伯	乐				
喘	气				
飞	奔				
任	何				
普	通				

仔	细				
确	实				
由	于				
强	壮				
果	然				
半	信	半	疑		

二　组字游戏

月 + 生 — □　　　口 + 山 + 而 — □

石 + 角 — □　　　弓 + 虽 — □

第九课 伯乐相马　　★ 练习一　　☆ 练习二　　☆ 练习三

三 在方框里找出6个词语，圈出来并写在空格里

强	壮	由	确
普	一	强	于
通	确	仔	实
一	由	实	细
段	仔	通	普

1. _____   2. _____

3. _____   4. _____

5. _____   6. _____

四 反义词填空

瘦弱——（　　）

仔细——（　　）

强壮	小心
粗心	强大

五 找出近义词

认真　　因为

仔细——　　　　　　由于——

第九课 伯乐相马

练习一　★练习二　☆练习三

一　量词连线

```
一段    衣服        一把    西瓜
一张    时间        一段    课文
一件    桌子        一个    椅子
```

二　根据课文判断对错

1. 春秋时期，有个叫伯乐的人很会看马。　　___对___错

2. 楚王请伯乐帮忙卖一匹千里马。　　　　　___对___错

3. 伯乐买了一匹拉车的瘦马给楚王。　　　　___对___错

4. 齐王看到瘦马很不高兴。　　　　　　　　___对___错

5. 马夫用心喂马，没多久马就强壮起来了。　___对___错

6. 楚王得到了千里马，打了很多胜仗。　　　___对___错

三　根据课文选择填空

1. _____请伯乐买一匹千里马。

　　A. 秦王　　　　B. 大王　　　　C. 楚王

第九课 伯乐相马

练习一 **练习二** 练习三

2. 一天，伯乐看见一匹马拉着车_____往山上走。

    A. 吃力地　　　　B. 飞快地　　　　C. 轻松地

3. 伯乐说这匹马_____是匹千里马。

    A. 可能　　　　　B. 确实　　　　　C. 不能

4. 楚王听了伯乐的话_____。

    A. 不信　　　　　B. 相信　　　　　C. 半信半疑

5. 人们用成语"伯乐相马"比喻_____。

    A. 会交朋友　　　B. 会发现人才

四　造句

  由于_____

  仔细_____

五　读课文两遍

第九课
伯乐相马

练习一　　练习二　　**练习三**

一　看图写话（两图各写一篇，每篇不少于4句）

　　提示：1. 两张图中哪一位是伯乐？

　　　　　2. 图1中，老人拿着放大镜看什么？

　　　　　3. 图2中，带黑眼镜的人摸着胖猪说什么？

　　　　图1　　　　　　　　　　　图2

图1 _____

_____

_____

图2 _____

_____

_____

第一课　听写

1.	2.	3.	4.
5.	6.	7.	8.
9.	10.	11.	12.

第三课　听写

1.	2.	3.	4.
5.	6.	7.	8.
9.	10.	11.	12.

第五课　听写

1.	2.	3.	4.
5.	6.	7.	8.
9.	10.	11.	12.

第七课　听写

1.	2.	3.	4.
5.	6.	7.	8.
9.	10.	11.	12.

第九课　听写

1.	2.	3.	4.
5.	6.	7.	8.
9.	10.	11.	12.

1.	2.	3.	4.
5.	6.	7.	8.
9.	10.	11.	12.

1.	2.	3.	4.
5.	6.	7.	8.
9.	10.	11.	12.

1.	2.	3.	4.
5.	6.	7.	8.
9.	10.	11.	12.

第九课　听写

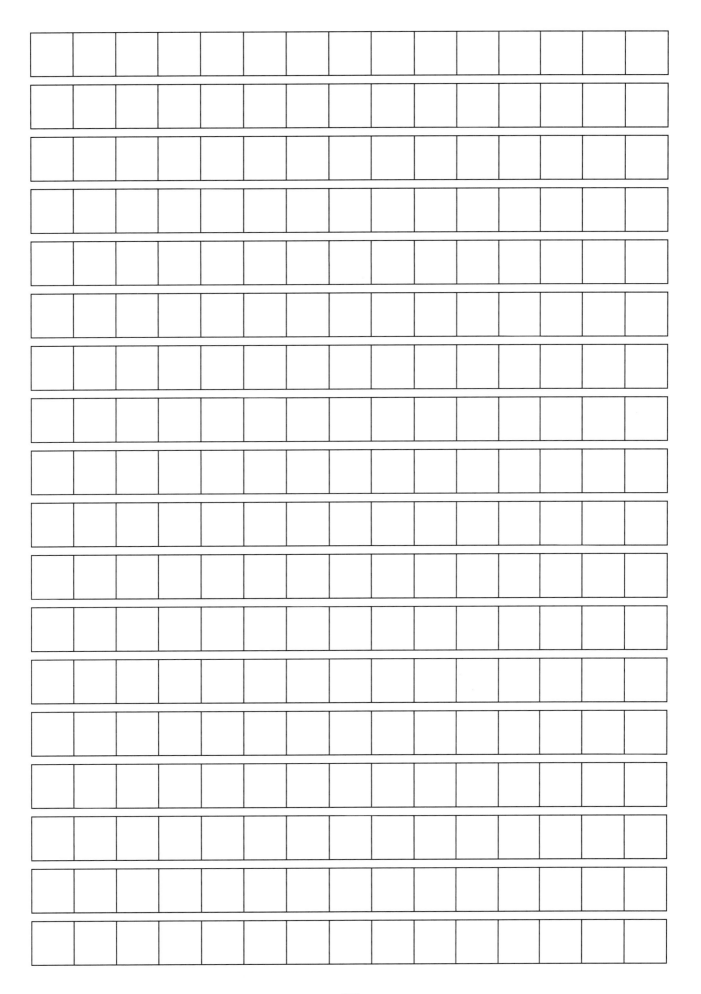

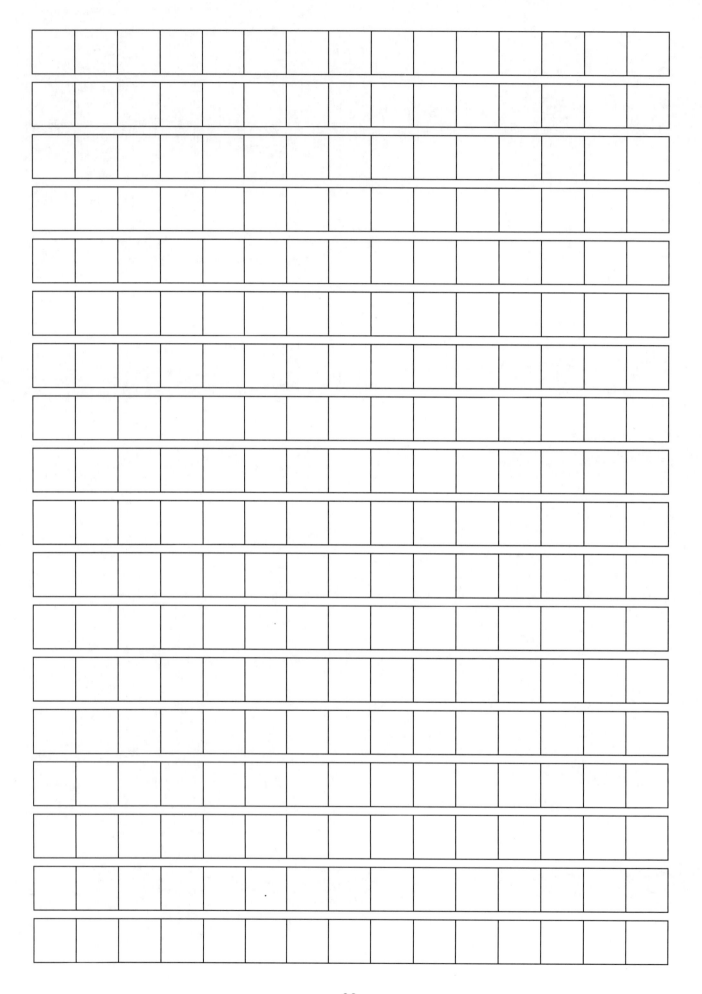

新双双中文教材 6
New Chinese Language and Culture Course

中国成语故事 Chinese Idiom Stories

练习本 双课

王双双 编著

北京大学出版社

目　录

第二课　　画蛇添足　…………………………………… 1

第四课　　滥竽充数　…………………………………… 6

第六课　　胸有成竹　竹文化　………………………… 11

第八课　　塞翁失马　…………………………………… 16

第十课　　愚公移山　…………………………………… 21

第二课 画蛇添足

练习一　　练习二　　练习三

一　写生词

添					
楚					
壶					
酒					
仆	人				
商	量				
其	中				

夺	过				
反	而				
多	余				
来	得	及			
得	意	洋	洋		

二　每字组两词

楚	清楚
	楚国

壶	

添	

商	

1

第二课 画蛇添足

练习一   练习二   练习三

三 选字组词

酒（壶 业）　　商（里 量）　　（旗 其）子

作（壶 业）　　仆（大 人）　　（旗 其）中

四 写出反义词

> 来不及　糊涂　主人

仆人_____　　来得及_____　　清楚_____

五 你在"量"字中，能看出几个字？

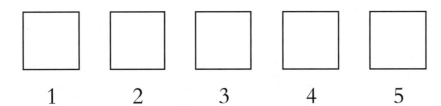

　1　　　2　　　3　　　4　　　5

六 根据课文选词填空

1. 哥哥起晚了，_____吃早饭了。（来不及　来得及）

2. 画蛇添足的人，_____没喝上酒。（反正　反而）

3. 一个楚国人给了他的仆人们一_____酒。（壶　盘）

4. 蛇是没有_____的。（却　脚）

第二课 画蛇添足

练习一　**练习二**　练习三

一　根据课文选择填空

1. 为了喝一壶酒，仆人们_____出一个办法。

    A. 大量　　　　B. 商量　　　　C. 力量

2. 有个人画得又快又好，他_____这壶酒一定是自己的了。

    A. 为了　　　　B. 因为　　　　C. 以为

3. 另一个人画完了蛇，_____酒壶。

    A. 夺过　　　　B. 端着　　　　C. 扔了

4. 最早画完蛇的人，_____给蛇添了脚，反而没有喝上酒。

    A. 虽然　　　　B. 但是　　　　C. 因为

二　造句

来得及_____

反而_____

第二课 画蛇添足

练习一　　★练习二　　练习三

三　看看"酒"字的演变，回答问题

甲骨文　　金文　　小篆　　楷体

1. 三千年前，中国人有了文字，叫甲骨文。甲骨文中有"酒"字。请写出甲骨文的"酒"字：☐

2. 两千多年前，中国人刻在铜器上的文字叫金文。金文中也有"酒"字。请写出金文的"酒"字：☐

3. 两千年前，中国人用的文字叫小篆。小篆中的"酒"字是这样：☐

四　写一写，上面的四个"酒"字，有没有相同的地方？你更喜欢哪个"酒"字，为什么？

_____

_____

_____

第二课 画蛇添足

练习一　　练习二　　**练习三**

一　看看画中车上装的是什么东西，写在方格中

 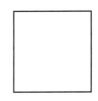

二　成语"画蛇添足"是说，做了多余的事情反而不好。英文中有没有相同意思的话？请写出来

_____

_____

三　根据阅读课文判断对错

1. 有个人想偷人家的铃铛。　　　　　　　___对___错

2. 他的办法是把自己的耳朵捂起来。　　　___对___错

3. 他把铃铛偷走了。　　　　　　　　　　___对___错

4. 想偷铃铛的人很聪明。　　　　　　　　___对___错

四　读课文两遍，讲一讲"画蛇添足"的故事

第四课 滥竽充数

练习一　　练习二　　练习三

一　写生词

战	国				
齐	国				
工	钱				
乐	手				
单	独				
根	本				

假	装				
周	围				
注	意				
偷	偷	地			
滥	竽	充	数		

二　读一读，并归类

假如　床单　足球队　单数　乐手
网球队　狐假虎威　假装　单人房
放假　吹竽队　单独　音乐　篮球队

1. 找出有"假"字的词 ＿＿＿ ＿＿＿ ＿＿＿ ＿＿＿

2. 找出有"单"字的词 ＿＿＿ ＿＿＿ ＿＿＿ ＿＿＿

3. 找出有"队"字的词 ＿＿＿ ＿＿＿ ＿＿＿ ＿＿＿

4. 找出有"乐"字的词 ＿＿＿ ＿＿＿ ＿＿＿ ＿＿＿

第四课 滥竽充数

练习一　　练习二　　练习三

三 写出反义词

> 单独　真实

一起——　　　　　　假装——

四 给多音字加拼音

1. 你喜欢音乐（　　）吗？

2. 祝你生日快乐（　　）！

五 根据课文选词填空

1. 南郭先生想_____吹竽队。（参加　进去）

2. 齐王给南郭先生很高的_____。（工钱　金银）

3. 南郭先生_____不会吹竽。（于是　根本）

4. 大家一起吹竽时，南郭先生_____吹竽。

（假装　真的）

5. 南郭先生害怕_____吹竽。（一起　单独）

第四课 滥竽充数 练习二

一 造句

根本＿＿＿＿＿＿＿＿＿＿＿＿＿＿＿＿＿＿＿＿＿＿＿＿

注意＿＿＿＿＿＿＿＿＿＿＿＿＿＿＿＿＿＿＿＿＿＿＿＿

二 看图练习描写细节

两位乐手怎样吹竽？结合提示词语判断谁是南郭先生。

提示：看看乐手的表情

眼睛　闭着　鼓着嘴　专心吹竽

东看西看　心神不定　假装在吹

＿＿＿＿＿＿＿＿＿＿＿＿＿＿＿＿＿＿＿＿＿＿＿＿＿＿
＿＿＿＿＿＿＿＿＿＿＿＿＿＿＿＿＿＿＿＿＿＿＿＿＿＿
＿＿＿＿＿＿＿＿＿＿＿＿＿＿＿＿＿＿＿＿＿＿＿＿＿＿
＿＿＿＿＿＿＿＿＿＿＿＿＿＿＿＿＿＿＿＿＿＿＿＿＿＿

第四课 滥竽充数

练习一　　练习二　　★ 练习三

一　看图选字写成语

热　能　生

熟　熊　巧

二　根据阅读课文《熟能生巧》选择填空

1. 从前，有一个人射箭_____。

　　A. 平常　　　　B. 百发百中　　　　C. 不错

2. _____的人都大声叫好。

　　A. 卖油　　　　B. 观看　　　　C. 会射箭

3. 一位卖油的老人只是_____。

　　A. 点了点头　　　　B. 生气　　　　C. 摇了摇头

第四课 滥竽充数

练习一　练习二　**练习三**

4. 老人往葫芦里倒油，油像_____一样流入葫芦。

　　A. 水　　　　　B. 丝绸　　　　　C. 细线

5. 老人说："也不过是_____。"

　　A. 熟能生巧　　B. 百发百中

三　"熟能生巧"的意思是熟练了就能有巧办法、好办法，你有没有这样的经验？

四　熟读课文两遍，体会成语"熟能生巧"

第六课 胸有成竹 竹文化

练习一　　练习二　　练习三

一 写生词

印				
夸				
房	屋			
无	论			
季	节			
深	深			
平	时			

出	现			
把	握			
胸	有	成	竹	
远	近	闻	名	

二 组字

王 + 见 — ☐　　　木 + 米 + 女 — ☐

工 + 力 — ☐　　　大 + 亏 — ☐

三 组词

季 _____　　平 _____　　屋 _____

李 _____　　苹 _____　　握 _____

第六课 胸有成竹 竹文化

练习一　★练习二　练习三

一 写生词

竹	筷

竹	笛

楼	

字	典

二 写出近义词

著名——　　　　　　　　　房子——

三 造句

平时_____

无论_____

四 根据《胸有成竹》选择填空

1. 北宋时有一位著名的_____叫文同。

　　A. 画家　　　　　B. 天文学家　　　　　C. 书法家

2. 每天都有不少人到文同家_____。

　　A. 卖画　　　　　B. 画画　　　　　C. 买画

第六课 胸有成竹 竹文化

练习一　　练习二　　练习三

3. 文同在自己家的房前房后种上_____的竹子。

　　A. 粗粗细细　　B. 各种各样　　C. 长长短短

4. _____春夏秋冬，文同都去竹林看竹子。

　　A. 平时　　B. 无论　　C. 出现

5. 后来人们用_____比喻做事之前已做好了准备。

　　A. 胸有成竹　　B. 滥竽充数　　C. 自相矛盾

五 根据《竹文化》回答问题

1. 在中国北方生长着许多竹子。　　___对___错

2. 中国人的生活离不开竹子。　　___对___错

3. 竹子也深入到中国的文化中。　　___对___错

4. "胸有成竹"就是一个成语。　　___对___错

5. 大熊猫最不喜欢吃竹子。　　___对___错

第六课 胸有成竹 竹文化

练习一 练习二 **练习三**

一 连一连

竹筷　　　　　　成语，用来比喻做事熟练，有把握。

竹楼　　　　　　用竹子做的小楼房，可以住人。

胸有成竹　　　　用竹子做的夹饭菜的细长棍儿。

竹笛　　　　　　一种用竹子做的中国乐器。

二 写出下列两本工具书的名字。如果想知道"守株待兔"的意思，应该用哪本？

1.＿＿＿＿＿＿　　　　2.＿＿＿＿＿＿

第六课
胸有成竹 竹文化

练习一　　练习二　　**练习三**

三　学习文同画竹

先画竹竿，再画竹叶，最后"胸有成竹"地画竹子。

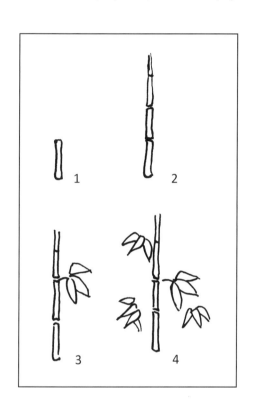

四　看图猜谜语（打一成语）

五　读课文两遍

第八课
塞翁失马

练习一　　　练习二　　　练习三

一　写生词

边	塞				
健	康				
损	失				
祝	贺				
担	心				
麻	烦				

战	场				
保	住				
性	命				
塞	翁	失	马		

二　组字

公 ＋ 羽 ＝ □　　　火 ＋ 页 ＝ □　　　加 ＋ 贝 ＝ □

三　组词

仗＿＿＿　姓＿＿＿　健＿＿＿　担＿＿＿

丈＿＿＿　性＿＿＿　建＿＿＿　但＿＿＿

四　每字组两词

保	

损	

命	

第八课 塞翁失马

练习一 **练习二** 练习三

一　写生词

摔	

断	

重	要

福	气

二　在方格中找出词语和成语

1. _____ 2. _____
3. _____ 4. _____
5. _____ 7. _____
7. _____ 8. _____
9. _____ 10. _____
11. _____

第八课 塞翁失马 练习二

三 根据课文完成句子

> 不一定是好事　损失不大　腿断了，却保住了命
>
> 好事有时可以变成坏事

1. 老人丢了一匹马，他说："＿＿＿＿＿＿。"

2. 老人的马又带回一匹好马，他说："＿＿＿＿＿＿。"

3. 老人的儿子骑马摔断腿，他说："＿＿＿＿＿＿
   ＿＿＿＿＿。"

4. "塞翁失马"比喻：坏事有时可以变成好事，＿＿＿＿
   ＿＿＿＿。

四 写出反义词

> 有病　丢掉　放心

担心—（　　　）　　保住—（　　　）　　健康—（　　　）

第八课 塞翁失马

练习三

一 造句

　　不但……而且……＿＿＿＿＿＿＿＿＿＿＿＿＿＿＿＿＿＿＿＿

二 读一读，画一画

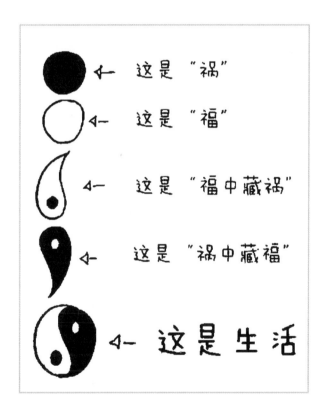

这是"祸"＿＿＿＿＿＿＿＿

这是"福"＿＿＿＿＿＿＿＿

这是"福中藏祸"＿＿＿＿＿＿

这是"祸中藏福"＿＿＿＿＿＿

这是生活＿＿＿＿＿＿＿＿

第八课 塞翁失马

练习一　练习二　**练习三**

三　写一写"塞翁失马"的故事，说明"福"和"祸"是可以相互转化的

_____
_____
_____
_____

四　读课文两遍

五　完成手工作业：自制成语小人书《塞翁失马》

　　要求：1. 画图并给图上色

　　　　　2. 写出图画内容

　　　　　3. 订成书保留

第十课 愚公移山

练习一　　练习二　　练习三

一　写生词

忍					
派					
方	便				
咱	们				
妇	女				
智	叟				

嘲	笑				
死	板				
顽	强				
忍	不	住			
愚	公	移	山		

二　给字加拼音，写出每组字中的相同部分，再组词

拼音（　　）（　　）　　（　　）（　　）（　　）

派　　旅　　　　朝　　嘲　　潮

□　　　　　　　□

组词

派_____　　　旅_____

朝_____　　　嘲_____　　　潮_____

21

第十课 愚公移山

练习一 ★

三 选字组词

方（便 更）　　（嘲 潮）笑　　（派 旅）人

（便 更）好　　（嘲 潮）湿　　（派 旅）行

四 根据课文选择填空

1. 愚公是一位老_____。

    A. 工人　　　B. 老师　　　C. 先生

2. 愚公要_____。

    A. 搬家　　　B. 移山　　　C. 爬山

3. 愚公的邻居是一个_____，她带着小儿子来了。

    A. 妇女　　　B. 农民　　　C. 将军

4. 智叟对愚公说："你太_____了。"

    A. 聪明　　　B. 糊涂　　　C. 马虎

5. 天帝被愚公的_____精神感动了。

    A. 死板　　　B. 顽强　　　C. 好学

第十课　愚公移山　　练习一　**练习二**　练习三

一　想一想为什么"愚、忍、感"三字下面都有"心"

　　　忍　　　　　感　　　　　愚

二　造句

方便＿＿＿＿＿＿＿＿＿＿＿＿＿＿＿＿＿＿＿＿＿＿＿＿＿

商量＿＿＿＿＿＿＿＿＿＿＿＿＿＿＿＿＿＿＿＿＿＿＿＿＿

三　连一连

塞翁失马　　　做事之前已有成功的把握

伯乐相马　　　做事不怕困难，一直做下去的精神

愚公移山　　　好事可以变成坏事，坏事可以变成好事

胸有成竹　　　比喻会发现人才

第十课 愚公移山　　练习二

四　看图给愚公和智叟写对话

智叟

愚公

第十课 愚公移山

练习一　　练习二　　**练习三**

一　看图写话

　　要求：1. 文章要分段　　2. 写出一些细节

_____

_____

_____

_____

二　想想在你的生活中，什么事情你坚持得最长

三　读课文两遍

第二课　听写

1.	2.	3.	4.
5.	6.	7.	8.
9.	10.	11.	12.

第四课　听写

1.	2.	3.	4.
5.	6.	7.	8.
9.	10.	11.	12.

第六课　听写

1.	2.	3.	4.
5.	6.	7.	8.
9.	10.	11.	12.

第八课　听写

1.	2.	3.	4.
5.	6.	7.	8.
9.	10.	11.	12.

第十课　听写

1.	2.	3.	4.
5.	6.	7.	8.
9.	10.	11.	12.

1.	2.	3.	4.
5.	6.	7.	8.
9.	10.	11.	12.

1.	2.	3.	4.
5.	6.	7.	8.
9.	10.	11.	12.

1.	2.	3.	4.
5.	6.	7.	8.
9.	10.	11.	12.

第十课　听写

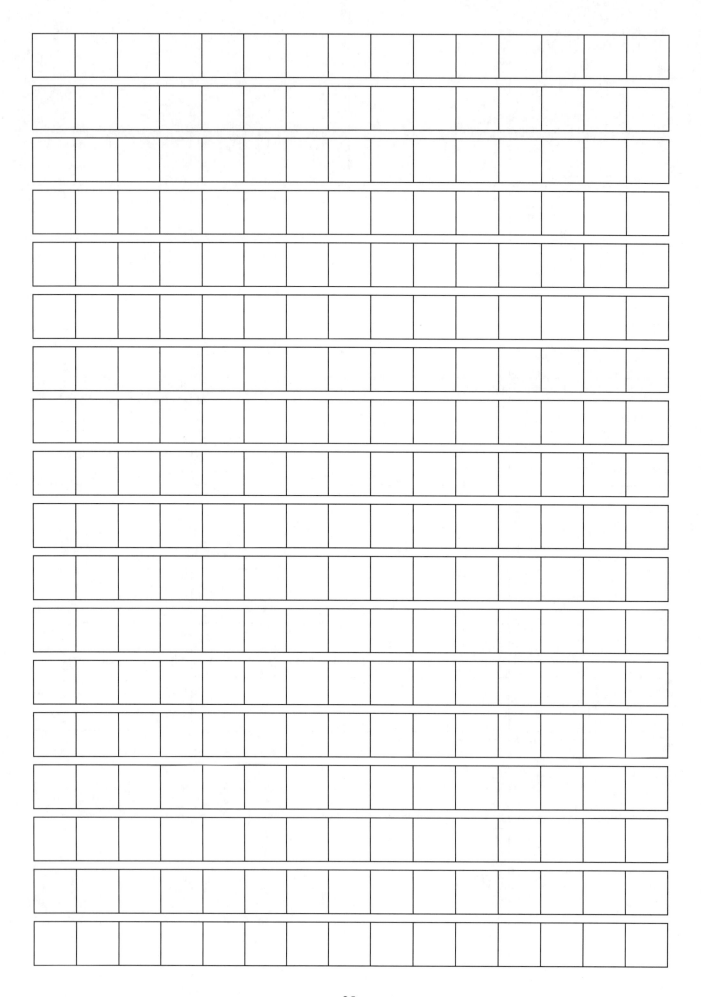